CORPORATE RISK MANAGEMENT

by

Professor. G. C. A. Dickson

Bowring Professor of Risk Management, Glasgow College

Chapters Six and Eight contributed by

Dr. W. J. Hastings

Chief Executive and Insurance Supervisor
The Isle of Man Insurance Authority
Douglas, Isle of Man

OTHER BOOKS IN THE SERIES

Business Finance for Risk Management

Liability Exposures

Physical Control of Risk

Risk Analysis

Risk and the Business Environment

Risk Financing

British Library Cataloguing in Publication Data
  Dickson, G.C.A.
  Corporate Risk Management
  1. Financial institutions. Risks. Management
  I. Title I. Institute of Risk Management

ISBN 0 948691 76 X

CORPORATE RISK MANAGEMENT

by

Professor G. C. A. Dickson
Professor of Risk Management Glasgow College

Chapters six and eight contributed by

Dr. W. J. Hastings
Chief Executive and Insurance Supervisor
The Isle of Man Insurance Authority
Douglas, Isle of Man

LONDON

WITHERBY & Co. Ltd.
32-36 Aylesbury Street
London EC1R 0ET

Published for:
The Institute of Risk Management

First Edition 1989
Reprinted 1995

©

Institute of Risk Management
and
Prof. G. C. A. Dickson
Dr. W. J. Hastings
1989

ISBN 0 948691 76 X

Printed and Published by

Witherby & Co. Ltd.
32-36 Aylesbury Street
London EC1R 0ET

Tel: 0171-251 5341
Fax: 0171-251 1296

INTRODUCTION

What is Risk Management? Is it risk identification and risk control? Is it a sophisticated form of insurance management or is it more to do with safety and loss control? What risk management means to each individual is probably dictated in large part by the attitude his company has or indeed the attitude the individual would like his company to have. There are so many different views and it is difficult to say which is correct and which is not. It would even be unwise to suggest that one method, successful in one situation, is a good model for the practice of risk management in a completely different environment.·

This does raise some difficult questions when it comes to writing a text which has the title 'Corporate Risk Management'. Is it possible to confine all that is involved in risk management to the pages of one relatively slim volume? Where should the emphasis be? What level of knowledge is implied before the reader comes to the book? and so on.

This text has been written with the needs of students in mind and particularly the needs of those who are studying for the Diploma of the Institute of Risk Management. As a result some of the problems associated with the scope of the book have been resolved but it is still necessary to state clearly what this book aims to do and, just as importantly, what its limitations are.

The first point to make is that this book should not be looked upon as a text book on all aspects of risk management. The reason for this is clear to see. Students of the Institute have studied or are studying eight other subjects ranging from Risk Analysis and Physical Control of Risk to Liability Exposures and Risk Financing. If this text on Corporate Risk Management covered the whole area of risk management there would have been little value in studying all these other subjects. As a result, those who come to this subject hoping that it will simply be a review of all that has gone before will be disappointed. A full knowledge of risk management is to be gained from combining all the relevant components of the individual subjects and applying them to the problems of risk.

It would also be wrong to think that the purpose of this subject, 'Corporate Risk Management', is to show the application of all that has been studied in earlier subjects. This would imply that no application, or at best limited application, of theory has been involved in earlier subjects. This is clearly not the case. In each of the earlier subjects, as in the texts, the application of concepts has been stressed. In fact in some cases the application of a concept has been stressed at the cost of a full treatment of the concept itself. This text, therefore, does not set out to repeat what has already been studied.

So much for what the book, and indeed the examination subject, is *not* about. What does the book intend to cover? The brief answer to this is that it intends to reflect the examination syllabus for the subject, as shown in the students' handbook. The syllabus is divided into seven sections and these seven sections are reflected in the chapters of this text. However, in an effort to set the scene for the study of risk management in a corporate sense, the first chapter sets out a summary of all that is involved in risk management.

In the syllabus, the first sections relate to the corporate role of risk management and the structure and administration of a risk management department. These managerial or administrative aspects of risk management are dealt with in chapter two.

There are two sections of the syllabus which deal with the important topic of decision making. We must not forget that the risk manager is a *manager* and one of the distinguishing characteristics of managers, as opposed to others in an organisation, is that they are required to make decisions. Chapters three, four and five look at the nature of risk management decisions and move on to examine the area of decision analysis.

Chapter six is concerned with forecasting in risk management. The whole of business is carried on in an environment of change and uncertainty and plans have to be made which take this into account. The chapter on forecasting is intended to provide readers with an intuitive grasp of what is an important and complex subject area.

Chapter seven introduces the international dimension which is becoming so common in most organisations. When an enterprise has an international aspect to its activities, special features of risk management have to be taken into account.

The final chapter of the book introduces a number of case studies. We have stressed that risk management is an inter-disciplinary subject. A number of different disciplines have to be combined in resolving most risk management problems. In order to illustrate this point, a number of case studies have been included which cover a range of different disciplines. At the end of each study some indication is provided as to the areas of knowledge which would be required to deal with the issues raised in the study.

The various techniques which are introduced in the text have merit in their own right but the reason for including them in the syllabus, and in the text, is not limited to their application. While there is indeed some intrinsic merit in all of the techniques covered in the book they also serve as a very useful discipline for the mind. It is hoped that in learning these concepts we have also, as a result, sharpened our analytical skills in general terms. It is always difficult to convince students of this point. There is an eagerness to confine one's learning only to that which can be applied directly in the short term. This line of thinking is not, however, terribly appropriate for the final subject in a post-experience course, such as the one being studied by the majority of those who will read this text.

In the end, students and other readers must take what they have learned from this text (if anything) and combine it with their own knowledge and experience. Then the real work of applying their understanding of corporate risk management can begin. Achieving a Diploma marks the end of one form of learning, it also acts as a starting point for the learning which will take place as theory is put into practice.

Prof. Gordon Dickson
Glasgow. 1989

CONTENTS

INTRODUCTION

Chapter 1

THE NATURE OF RISK MANAGEMENT

1.0 What is risk? This may seem a strange question to ask in the final text book of a Diploma in Risk Management. However, if we are to understand the corporate role which risk management can play in organisations we must be clear in our mind as to what we mean by risk itself.

Someone once said that risk was the sugar and salt of life. This is an excellent definition of what risk is all about. Risk brings sweetness to life and it brings bitterness. Few of us would want a world totally free of risk. There is something exciting about risk, an edge which it brings, a dimension we would not want to give up. The other side of risk is less attractive. The bitter side of risk is one with which we are only too familiar. It is this 'downside' of risk which concerns us in our studies and work.

'Risk' is the unlooked for, unwanted event in the future. There have been many examples in recent years. The man in the street would be able to name quite a number of events which he would consider to be 'risks'. He may head his list with events such as those at Flixborough, Seveso, Three Mile Island, Bhopal, Chernobyl, Zeebrugge, Piper Alpha or Kings Cross. These events, and others like them have certainly grabbed the headlines but they are only the tip of the risk iceberg. They are the events which make the headlines and the news bulletins but they are far removed from the everyday forms of risk which regularly confront us. The 'real' level of risk comprises the steady toll of fires, accidents, thefts, explosions and other similar events. These are events which rarely grab front page space in our newspapers but nevertheless from the bulk of the work of risk management. Those who have read *Risk Analysis*, also published for the Institute of Risk Management, were given some feel for the reality of risk in the United Kingdom at least. For as long as we have fire costs running at several hundred million pounds per year, have almost forty road casualties every hour, kill two people at work every day and pay out over two hundred and fifty million pounds to those injured at work, then there is a need for effective management of risk.

1.1 The Meaning of Risk Management

Before going any further let us define what we mean by risk management. The text books are full of definitions of risk management and everyone who has thought about it will have their own. It would be interesting to make a list of all the answers people might give if they were asked to say what they thought of risk management. The list may well include the following statements:

- It's what we have been doing for years anyway.
- We could never afford to have a risk manager.
- It's only what a good broker would do for you anyway.
- It is not appropriate for our size of company.
- It is in direct competition with insurance.
- It's an essential part of management.
- It's just a gimmick.
- It's only common sense.
- It is no more than good insurance management.

1

- It just takes commission away from brokers.
- It's just a fancy name for safety management.

We said earlier that risk was about the unfortunate things which may happen in the future. Risk management is about recognising what these events are, how severe they may be and how they can be controlled. A working definition of risk management could be:

"The identification, analysis and economic control of those risks which can threaten the assets or earning capacity of an enterprise."

Notice one or two important points about this definition:

1. The three-fold approach to risk management is quite evident. Risks must be indentified before they can be measured and only after their impact has been assessed can we decide what to do with them.

2. The eventual control mechanism, whatever it is, must be 'economic'. There is no point is spending ten pounds to control a risk which can only ever cost you five. There will always be a point where spending on risk control has to stop.

3. The definition mentions assets and earning capacity. These assets can of course be physical or human. They are both important and risk management must be seen to have a part to play in both. However, risks do not only strike at assets directly and for this reason the definition mentions the earning capacity of an enterprise.

4. Finally, note that the definition uses the word 'enterprise' rather than a more restrictive word such as 'company' or 'manufacturer'. The principles of risk management are just as applicable in the service sector as the manufacturing sector and are of equal importance in the public and private sectors of the economy.

1.2   The Response to Risk

In this chapter we will take each of the three main strands of the definition, identification, analysis and control and expand on it. However, let us pause to ask what response management has made in the past to the problems posed by risk. Clearly this is highly subjective and each reader will have his own view, largely determined by his personal experiences. Being critical, we would have to say that general management has not been too responsive to risk. This is probably understandable:

- Insurance was always thought to be the answer to risk. When premiums were low there was no incentive to think about risk in terms other than the cost of the insurance premium. However in a hardening market and with increasing capacity problems, an incentive did emerge to think about containing insurance costs.

- General management suffered, in the same way as the general public, from the *'it won't happen to me syndrome'*. This is fairly common among the population at large and there is no reason to believe that it is any less prevalent among business managers. How often have you sat across the desk from someone knowing that he thinks himself to be immune to whatever event it is you are describing?

- During the years when current senior managers were being groomed, there was an element of financial fat in the land, fat which has not been apparent over recent years. During certain periods of our business history, rather less attention was paid to items of expenditure than is the case today. When this was the case the real cost of insurance would rarely be questioned.

- One final factor which may account for the low response to risk is the whole question of schooling. Very few school children ever see the inside of a factory while at school. This is changing now, but for those who currently hold positions of responsibility it is likely that they completed their entire schooling without visiting any industrial or commercial premises. Linked to this is the almost certain fact that 'risk' would not have been mentioned in the classroom. Each reader can answer this point for themselves, was risk ever the subject of a lesson, project, discussion at school? Most of us will have completed our schooling in an unreal environment where events either definitely happened or did not happen — risk played no part. Little wonder that when we achieve adulthood we find it difficult to separate the real from the perceived level of risk.

The tide has been changing over recent years and we have seen a far more positive attitude to risk being developed and through it all, risk management has developed as an integrated approach to risk. There are now over six hundred members of the professional body of risk managers. The Association of Insurance and Risk Managers in Industry and Commerce, AIRMIC. Around sixty four percent of the top one hundred companies in the United Kingdom have risk managers and this growth has been repeated in many parts of the world.

1.3   Risk Identification

In thinking of risk identification we must remember to take the broad view. We are not solely concerned with what can be insured, or even with what can be controlled. We start from the very basic question of, "How can the assets or earning capacity of the enterprise be threatened?" Starting from this position does not place any constraint on us as to what kind of risks we are looking for. We must begin the task in an unblinkered manner, willing to identify the whole host of ways in which an organisation may be impeded in achieving its objectives.

This is very much easier to say than to put into practice. In a fictional sense it would be ideal if a gantry could be built above the open-roofed buildings which contain our company. If it were possible to do so then we would be able to walk along the gantry and see down into all the compartments which make up the organisation. We would be able to identify what was done in each compartment, how the process in one area was potentialy dangerous to the compartment next to it. We would be able to see how each section of the company interacted, where the points of possible conflict emerged, where concentrations of processes existed, whether there were any dependencies etc. Not only would we be able to look down on our company, we would also be able to look outside the plant itself and see the ways in which what we were doing could be a threat to the surrounding neighbour-hood and hence a potential risk to us. We could also see if there was someone close by who was a potential threat to us.

3

If we could be up there on that gantry we would see all forms of risk and not just those which we knew to be insurable or those we had some experience of in the past. For example, the company which had been storing all its finished stock in the one finished goods store would be able to see the problems which this would pose in the event of a fire or flood or some other form of loss or dàmage to stock. The company whose three production lines all depend on the one packaging machine would be helped to see the unwise level of dependency inherent in the system. The company with several manufacturing plants, but with the production of its most profitable product limited to one plant, would see the risks associaed with this concentration of activity. *"Common sense"* you may say, *"no need for any fancy form of risk identification, anyone would be able to see these risks!"* Common sense it may be but each of these examples is based on fact. What we would hope is that by some form of rigorous risk identification the whole spectrum of risk, as shown in Fig 1.1 would lie before us.

Fig 1.1

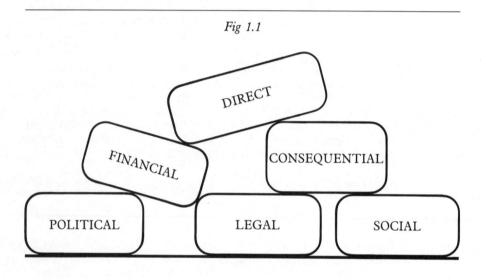

This may be a fine idea but it is only theory! We can see the benefits but how can they be achieved in reality? How can this fictional idea be transformed into reality? In the end we could say that there are at least two essentials if risk identification is to be effective.

1. The task of risk identification must be someone's job

   Managers within the company are busy managing finance, production, marketing, sales and so on. We cannot rely on somebody identifying risk unless it is spelled out that it is part of their function. In many firms this will mean a risk manager but in others, which may not be large enough to have a risk manager, it may mean that someone's job description includes the identification of risk.

   The events at Flixborough are a good example of the value of having someone defined to be the risk indentification person. Prior to the explosion at Flixborough one of a set of chemical reactors had been removed for repair. In order to keep production flowing it had been decided to install a dog-leg pipe around the damaged reactor. A flange used to connect this pipe did not prove strong enough and the result is well known. The official enquiry into all the facts surrounding the explosion makes very interesting reading for anyone involved in risk management. One passage from that report is particularly relevant to what we are saying at the moment, it reads:

"The key post of works engineer was vacant and none of the senior personnel, who were chemical engineers, were capable of recognising the existence of what in essence was a simple engineering problem."

One could interpret this as meaning that nobody had the specific task of asking how the changes in the plant had altered the risks inherent in its operation.

You may say that common sense should have been applied. The same charge could also be levied in respect of other major incidents, Chernobyl and Zeebrugge to name only two. It is clear from the history of major losses that common sense is often not applied. Someone has to be responsible for risk identification and know that he is responsible.

2. The tools of risk identification must be available to the person whose job it is to identify risk.

There is much more to identifying risk than the walk round a factory. Earlier texts in the Diploma of the Institute of Risk Management have dealt with the detail of risk identification and analysis. There are a number of techniques, each having its own role to play. Some of these are shown in Fig 1.2

Fig 1.2

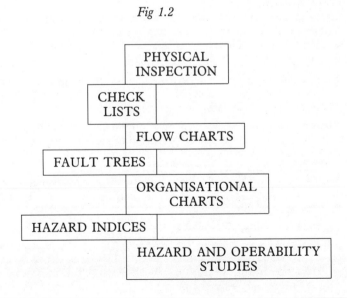

1.4   Risk Analysis

Once the risk has been identified the next task is to measure the impact you feel it will have on the enterprise. This inevitably takes us into the realm of quantitative analysis and many people begin to feel a little uncomfortable.

What we want to do is to measure how important the risk is to us in financial terms. Is it one which can be assumed by the company at very little cost or is it one which is of catastrophic proportions? Without going into the detail of analysis, and repeating what has gone before, we could say that at least three points should be borne in mind.

1. The detail of what has happened in the past is a good starting point for any analysis of what might happen in the future. A loss experience can yield interesting information on the trend and pattern of losses. The widespread use of the microcomputer has been a great boon in this task. Where data on previous losses has been stored it can then be retrieved in any order. Losses at one plant, involving one type of injury and those of a certain age group can be found at the press of a button, assuming the correct information was fed into the computer in the first place (garbage in garbage out?).

    Trends can become apparent which hitherto would have been hidden in the data simply because the task of sorting claims would have been so time consuming.

2. Losses must the thought of in terms of their impact on the organisation. In a very basic way we can identify the "layers" of our losses. There would be the bottom layer which is characterised by high frequency and low severity. This layer is often referred to as the pound swapping layer as the losses are predictable. The insurer and the insured know that losses in this region will occur. The insured pays the premium and in due course has the inevitable losses met. Unfortunately from the insured's point of view, the insurer has had to have all its expenses met and a profit returned on the transaction. These are the losses which may wipe us out if they occurred. In the centre we have the middle layer of losses of medium severity and moderate frequency.

    Expressing our losses in terms of these layers helps us to understand the impact of the losses and could be a pointer to assist in the risk financing decisions which may have to be taken.

3. The final point to remember is that your analysis of loss may in the end have to be read by someone else or presented to someone in the form of a report. It is essential that we express our losses or potential losses, the impact of risk, in a way which is understood by those with whom we must work. We may be speaking to plant managers, finance managers, general managers and hence we must be able to communicate our findings in a way which they will find understandable.

    We could, for example, express our employee injury costs in terms of lost profit. We will be able to find out what the profit margin on each unit produced is and we can then express the loss costs either in terms of units of production or in lost profit e.g. We have to sell three hundred tables each month simply to pay for the injury claims. Or, £x hundred pounds worth of tables have to be sold each month just to meet injury claims.

1.5   Risk Control

The final step in the process of managing risk is that of economic control. Let us just emphasise that we are only concerned with economic control. A corner shop could be protected in such a way as to reduce the risk of fire to an absolute minimum, but the cost of doing so may use up an entirely unreasonable percentage of the shop's turnover. We must be financially reasonable in the steps we recommend. We can think of control in three ways.

1.5.1   Reduction

The first step in any loss control programme must be that of reduction. We must make sure that the risk is as low as we can possibly make it. There is a great tendency to rush on to the step of controlling by insurance, without first exhausting all possible ways of reducing the impact of the loss. Reduction of loss can take place before or after the event has taken place.

Pre-loss reduction involves those steps which the risk manager would think of taking once a risk has been identified but prior to any loss occurring. Instructions issued with a product would constitute a form of pre-loss reduction. The manufacturer has identified the risk that a consumer may cause himself injury and so issues instructions in the hope that such events can be avoided.

Unfortunately it is still too often the case that the risk management department does not have the opportunity to take pre-loss risk reduction steps. Often the risk manager will hear of some new development or process after it has been installed. His scope for pre-loss reduction is then limited. The ideal situation is that the risk manager is one of the group of managers which examines all new proposals. This depends on the corporate philosophy towards risk management but severe restrictions are placed on the effectiveness of risk management if the risk manager is not involved at an early stage in company projects.

Post-loss reduction involves those steps which the risk manager believes will reduce the impact of the loss once the event has taken place. The use of fire sprinkler systems is a good example of this kind of thinking. Once the event has occurred the sprinklers are intended to drastically reduce its impact.

The whole area of risk reduction is one where the risk manager requires a great deal of skill. The knowledge he has of the processes carried out within his company must be combined with his understanding of the physical means by which risk can be controlled. In a real sense he must integrate all the pieces of information he has in order to arrive at the optimum solution.

1.5.2   Retention

Once the risk has been identified and reduced as far as possible, the decision has to be taken as to what is now to be done. Again, there is a tendency to rush to the step of transferring the risk to some other party like an insurer. Before transferring the risk, which must cost us something, let us firstly satisfy ourselves that we cannot simply retain the risk.

Losses which are expected to be in the pound swapping layer which we talked about earlier will be expensive to transfer to some insurer. The insurer will want the claims cost covered and in addition will have its own expenses and profit to

7

meet. Losses in this bottom layer may well be suitable for retention. The risk manager will not want to expose his company to an intolerable level of loss nor does he want to spend money on insurance which may not be justified. A whole host of mechanisms can be called on in such situations.

However, this is not to imply that all decisions about retaining risk are taken voluntarily by the risk manager. In some cases the retention of risk may be involuntarily thrust upon the risk manager. For example, there may be limited capacity for a certain form of risk and the risk manager is left carrying some himself. In other cases the cost of cover may simply be prohibitive, thus forcing the risk manager to consider some alternative.

1.5.3   Transfer

The final step in the process is that of risk transfer. Essentially what the risk manager is trying to do is to transfer the risk to some other party. This may be done by wording a contract in such a way as to leave any risk with the other party. However, the most common form of risk transfer is by insurance.

As far as the risk manager is concerned, insurance is simply a risk transfer mechanism. He incurs a certain loss today, the insurance premium, and is relieved of the uncertainty as to how costly any future losses will be. The great benefit of insuring is that loss costs are fixed, or almost fixed. This allows for easier budgeting as the loss costs are smoothed over the year rather than occurring at random.

1.6   Conclusion

This brief summary of the process of risk management is intended to set the scene for all that is to follow in the remainder of this text. Many of the actual techniques of risk management have been dealt with elsewhere in the syllabus of the Institute and we move on now to pick up one or two topics of a more corporate nature.

Chapter 2

CORPORATE RISK MANAGEMENT

2.0   In Chapter One we looked, in brief, at the whole process of risk management. We saw that risk management is not one subject alone, it is the aggregate of very many different disciplines. Even the use of the word *aggregate* is not accurate as this would imply a simple addition of different subjects. In fact, risk management is more properly described as a *function* of many disciplines. It takes what is valuable from a number of different areas and blends them together in such a way as to produce a new subject out of the parts. This may seem a very long way of justifying a subject on risk management! What the Institute of Risk Management's Diploma syllabus has done is to provide all the technical aspects of risk management in earlier subjects, in addition to a measure of integration. At the end of the syllabus it is important to pull everything together and add some additional material which is necessary in order to round off the reader's education.

In this chapter we turn to the more corporate, managerial aspects of risk management and build on all that we already know. The chart in Fig 2.1 is an attempt at illustrating the function of risk management. This is not a chart of how to carry out effective risk management but is more a chart of the process by which risk management can be implemented.

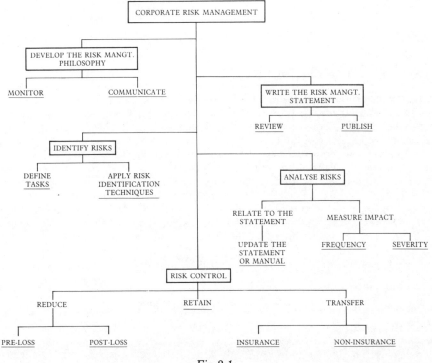

Fig 2.1

We can see from the chart the familiar steps of risk identification, analysis and control. These steps were all mentioned in chapter one and dealt with individually in the various subjects of the Institute's Diploma syllabus. What the chart reveals is that before these steps can be carried out there is the task of developing the risk management philosophy and writing the risk management statement. In this chapter we will concentrate on these preliminary areas of risk management. In later chapters we consider the whole subject of decision making for risk management, in its many forms.

The process by which a particular risk manager decides to manage risks varies enormously from person to person. It is not possible to say that there is one best method for doing any single job. What we can do perhaps is to suggest what the alternatives are and list various advantages and disadvantages. In this chapter we will be concerned with administering a risk management programme, in the broadest sense. For our purposes we will split the task into three:

● The work of the risk manager
● The work of the risk management department
● The structure and location of the risk management department.

The chief reason for making this split is so that we can separate the policy making or strategic functions of the risk manager from the implementation of that policy. We will look at policy making as a responsibility of the risk manager and implementation as the work of the department. This may not be a reasonable split or even one that will be visible in the real world but it is intended to assist our understanding of all that is involved in being a risk managser and in running a risk management department.

2.1   The Risk Manager

There is an increasing number of job adverts for risk managers appearing in the press and from them it is possible to conclude that very many different things are expected of the risk manager. One thing is sure and that is that the title does not necessarily give any real indication of the job the manager is expected to perform. To illustrate this point we can look at the 1987 survey carried out by AIRMIC, The Association of Insurance and Risk Managers in Industry and Commerce, into the status of its members. In that survey only 10.6% of all respondents were termed *risk managers*, while over 64% were *insurance managers*. What is interesting is to look at the change which has taken place over the last ten years in the designations used to describe those involved in risk management. The figures in the table below represent the proportion of respondents having the corresponding job title.

TITLE	1977	1981	1983	1985	1987
Insurance	76.8	77.9	72.8	71.3	64.8
Insurance and Risk	2.8	4.7	5.9	6.3	11.3
Risk Management	4.2	6.1	5.3	7.5	10.6

The change is quite clear. In 1977 only seven percent of those who responded to the AIRMIC survey had the word *RISK* in their job title. Ten years later this percentage had increased to almost twenty two.

In the end it is not terribly important what title a person has, although it has to be said that some people attach a certain kudos to some titles as opposed to others! It is the nature of the work itself which is important and this cannot be measured accurately from the title.

We have singled out five aspects of his work, remembering that we are concerned at the moment with broad policy making matters as opposed to the practical steps of actually implementing the policy.

2.1.1 He is a manager

The first and most obvious aspect of the risk manager's job is that he is a manager. He must manage his department just as any other manager manages a department. This means he has certain responsibilities:

- Economic performance. Peter Druker, a prolific writer and scholar on management wrote once that, *"It (management) can only justify its existence and its authority by the economic results it produces."* This is as true for the risk manager as it is for any other manager and means that targets have to be met, budgets adhered to and decisions followed.

- Specific tasks. In addition to these general responsibilities the risk manager has specific responsibilities for his own department. On top of the business of setting general policy in the field of risk management he will also have to concern himself with the problems of staff management, staff training, motivation and the many aspects of management.

2.1.2 The risk management philosophy

The risk management philosophy should be the one clear statement of where the company stands on the issue of risk and its management. It is often expressed in the form of a risk management statement and we will look at this next. Deciding on a corporate philosophy towards risk does bring with it a number of distinct advantages:

(i) It means that the long term objectives of risk management are thought out by the company. Rather than respond to incidents as and when they occur, the company has declared what it believes to be the optimum approach given the information it has. In this way the company is seen to be positive in its attitude to risk rather than just responsive when needs must.

(ii) Declaring a philosophy does focus attention on the work of the risk management department. This can be no bad thing when the risk manager is trying to get people to think positively about the problems posed by risk. The company is likely to have a declared philosophy in a number of areas from marketing to product design, investment to diversification. Placing a risk management philosophy alongside all these others could heighten the profile of risk management and bring with it an increased awareness of risk itself.

(iii) The philosophy can also act as a useful benchmark against which to measure the effectiveness of the risk manager and his department. Where no philosophy has been made known then it would be very difficult for the risk manager or his superiors to know if he is performing a satisfactory job. The task of measuring effectiveness would become very subjective and personal.

The philosophy will not overcome subjective assessments of performance or remove the issue of personality from any discussions but it will provide a useful measuring stick.

(iv) The philosophy will also outlive any one risk manager and therefore represent the corporation's view of the management of risk rather than the thoughts of one individual alone. This is essential if long term planning is to take place and the management of risk evolve within the company as a whole. Too many people have their own firm view on one or other aspect of risk management and given no restraints they may wish to have their own ideas become the philosophy of the company. A permanent philosophy attempts to overcome these problems. It is not permanent in the sense that it is inflexible but is permanent in the sense that it is the corporate view, out-living the period of employment of any one individual.

(v) One final point worth making is that the generating of the philosophy should certainly have involved a number of executives within the organisation. This can be no bad thing if the risk manager is still in the business of increasing the profile of the risk management department. The work he will have to have carried out with a number of executives represents good public relations, or could represent good public relations provided it is done properly.

2.1.3   The risk management statement

Let us leave the issue of the philosophy, which many may have considered as rather theoretical, and move on to the more practical point of the risk management statement. The statement is a policy document in which broad issues are set out. It is not a manual in the sense of telling the reader *how* something is to be done, this will come later in the actual risk management manual. Ideally the statement should be brief and to the point, two examples are shown in Figs 2.2 and 2.3.

Fig 2.2

IMPERIAL MACHINES PLC

It is the policy of this company to take all reasonable steps in the management of pure risk, to ensure that the company is not financially or operationally disrupted.

In implementing this general philosophy, it is the policy of the company to:

1. Identify those activities which have or may give rise to loss producing events.

2. Measure the impact of potential loss producing events on the company and its subsidiaries.

3. Take reasonable physical or financial steps to avoid or reduce the impact of potential losses.

4. Purchase insurance for those risks which cannot be avoided or reduced further, always retaining risk where this is economically attractive.

Fig 2.3

ASSOCIATED PLANT LIMITED

The Risk Management Department is responsible for implementing all Risk Management activities. It has specified responsibilities in the areas of:

Risk Identification
Risk Evaluation
Insurance

The Risk Management Department will act in an advisory capacity in the areas of:

Physical Loss Prevention

The Department will co-ordinate the activities of safety, occupational health and other related matters.

Fig 2.2 illustrates a relatively brief statement. It is very much slanted towards the objectives of the department, for example "identify activities", "measure impact", "take reasonable steps", "purchase insurance". These all relate to the work of the department and so we can say that the statement is objectives centred. This is not necessarily a bad thing but it simply represents one style. While being fairly oriented to objectives it is quite wide in its remit. We could not say that it is in any way restrictive on the actions of the risk manager or his department. The opposite could almost be the case. The statement is very wide and its liberal use of such words as "loss producing events", "reasonable" and "economically attractive" all give the risk manager a good measure of flexibility. The statement can also be seen to follow fairly closely the three main steps in risk management of identification, analysis and control and this may be wise if the statement is to be read by large numbers of people outside the risk management fraternity.

The sample statement in Fig 2.3, by comparison, is quite a different style. In this illustration we have a very brief statement which avoids specifics but stresses the co-ordinating role of the risk manager and his department. There are clearly a large number of variations in the way that statements can be written and each organisation has to decide on the style which is most suited to its organisation, bearing in mind the normal style of other statements within the organisation and the general corporate structure.

A third example of a risk management statement is shown in Fig 2.4. This has been extracted from a fairly recent book on the practical aspects of risk management, *Avoiding Surprises* written by F. C. Church Jnr. and published by The Boston Risk Management Corporation. The extract is included with the kind permission of the publisher.

Fig 2.4

INSURANCE AND RISK MANAGEMENT POLICY STATEMENT

Our organization is exposed to various risks which may be insured or not insured. We may also control these risks through our loss control program.

The objective of our insurance and risk management program is to preserve our assets and earnings. The following policy has been prepared with this in mind:

   a. We will identify sources of loss to our property, our net income, our employees, and the general public.

   b. We will evaluate the impact of loss in terms of frequency and severity.

   c. We will make every effort to control the causes of loss by and through our loss control program.

   d. We will retain risks whenever the amount of potential loss would not significantly affect our assets and earnings.

   e. We will purchase insurance in such amounts and in such areas as will provide assurance against catastrophe loss and where insurance is required by law or contractual agreement; when desirable services are obtained from the insurance carrier; and when the degree of risk, compared with the cost of insurance, dictates the economic feasibility of purchasing insurance coverage.

   f. In recognition of our financial resources and the location of our physical assets, the organization is able to accept retention of uninsured losses as follows:

- Not more than $_____ arising out of a single event or occurrence.

- Not more than $_____ aggregate during any fiscal year.
  Deductibles of less than $_____ will be purchased only when dictated by:

- Cost/benefit comparisons.

- Legal or contractual requirements.

- Desirable insurance carrier services.

What can we say is the value of these written statements?

- They are a way of communicating the philosophy of the company as far as risk management is concerned. The best philosophy in the world will be of no value at all if it is not communicated to those who are meant to implement it.

- The statement can also encourage an element of corporate discussion around the problems of risk and its management. Provided this is constructive discussion, it is a good thing.

- The statement will probably show the lines of authority. It will state who is responsible for certain aspects of the management of risk. At the same time it can also be used to say what areas of risk management are the responsibility of others outside the risk management department. For example the statement may make it clear that all acquisitions are to be reported to the risk manager by divisional general managers.

2.1.4   The risk management manual

We have already said that the risk management statement is not the same as the manual. The statement outlines the policy of the company towards the problem of risk whereas the manual actually sets out the practice which the company wishes to see implemented. The manual therefore becomes the *how* of risk managsement covering points such as who is to notify losses, the insurance regulations, what to do in the event of a loss etc., etc.

Why go to the bother of preparing such a manual? Many risk managers do without one and manage well enough. What are the advantages of a manual?

- We could say firstly that it does represent all the practical information relevant to risk in the one resource book.

- The responsibilities of all the various parties can be stated quite clearly. This means the responsibilities of both the risk manager and others.

- Ambiguities in practice can be avoided if the position on a number of key issues is stated clearly. It can often be the case that there is some ambiguity about who is to report a certain type of incident in the event of a loss, or who is to be informed if new machinery is purchased. The manual can lay out the lines of communication quite clearly.

- Specific points about policies of insurance could be made clear, for example who is permitted to drive company vehicles, or what medical cover applies for employees travelling abroad etc.

- The manual can also act as a useful reference work on such issues as fire, explosions, industrial diseases etc.

To be quite realistic we would have to say of course that all these advantages will only accrue if people use the manual. The relative lack of use of manuals of this kind may well be attributed to a large measure of scepticism as to their *practical* value. Assuming we would like to explore the idea of a manual further, and given that we are reading this text as students, let us examine the possible contents of a manual!

Just as with the statement there can be a wide variation in style of manual. Ideally the manual should be a document which is regularly up-dated and as such a loose-leaf style of production would probably be best. As to the actual contents then we might suggest that the following should be included:

The risk management philosophy, or the statement, if this is a more appropriate wording.

Loss prevention
Details on fire, security, safety etc. could be provided so that all the relevant people would be in no doubt as to what was expected of them in so far as prevention was concerned.

Any specific insurance regulations concerned with loss prevention could be stated e.g. removal of waste from the premises, use of machine guards etc.

Insurance provision
Explain what is covered and more importantly what is not insured.

Outline the responsibility of those who are to inform the risk management department of changes in plant etc.

Explain any areas which commonly cause trouble or have been the source of questions in the past e.g. who can drive a company car, what cover applies to personal effects etc.

CORPORATE RISK MANAGEMENT

Loss reporting
What is to be reported.

Who is to report it.

When it is to be reported.

Provide sample forms, outlining how they are to be completed.

General issues
Foreign travel, one off ventures, trials, exhibitions etc.

The point of contact within the risk management department.

The procedure in the event of mergers or acquisitions.

The manual can be an effective tool for the risk manager if it is constructed properly and in fact used by those to whom it is issued. If it is not used properly then the whole exercise will be a total waste of time. On balance it is certainly better to have a manual which is well used than not to have one at all, the only problem which remains is to see that it is in fact used!

In Fig 2.5 we show an example of a full manual, again extracted from *Avoiding Surprises*. You can see that this is fairly comprehensive and goes into the detail of what is to be reported in the event of losses of different types, it defines certain terms which the layman may find helpful, it explains what information is to be provided to the risk manager in the event for example of new exposures etc., etc.

Fig 2.5

MATERIAL COVERED IN INSURANCE AND RISK MANAGEMENT MANUAL

Section   Subject

I.   Manual Purpose

II.   Insurance and Risk Management Policy Statement
Loss Control Policy Statement
Risk Management Department
Outside Vendors
Emergency Telephone Numbers
Corporate Indemnification
Uninsured Exposures

III. Claims

IV.   Basic Insurance Buying Guidelines

V.   Risk Management Definitions
Experience Rating and Retrospective Rating

VI.   New Exposures
New Construction
Inspections
Surety Bonds

16

Contractors
Requests for Certificates of Insurance
Hold Harmless Agreements
Leases

VII.   Reporting of Values
Audits
Allocations
Personal Property of Employees
Employee Use of Company Owned/Leased Automobiles
Rented Automobiles
Employee Use of Aircraft and Watercraft
Key Executives in Single Aircraft
Product Recall
Household Goods in Transit
Kidnap and Ransom
Travel in War-Risk Zones
Other

VIII.   Insurance Policy Description

SECTION I

Manual Purpose
This manual outlines our organization's policy toward the management of fortuitous losses to which we are exposed as a result of our everyday activities.

It is the purpose of this manual to contribute to proper risk management by providing information on our risk management program, organization, and procedures.

SECTION II

Insurance and Risk Management Policy Statement
Our organization is exposed to various risks which may be insured or not insured. We may also control these risks through our loss control program.

The objective of our insurance and risk management program is to preserve our assets and earnings. The following policy has been prepared with this in mind:

a. We will identify sources of loss to our property, our net income, our employees, and the general public.

b. We will evaluate the impact of losses in terms of the frequency and severity.

c. We will make every effort to control the causes of loss by and through our loss control program.

d. We will retain risks whenever the amount of potential loss would not significantly affect our assets and earnings.

e. We will purchase insurance in such amounts and in such areas as will provide assurance against catastrophe loss and where insurance is required by law or contractual agreement; when desirable services are obtained from the insurance carrier; and when the degree of risk, compared with the cost of insurance, dictates the economic feasibility of purchasing insurance coverage.

f. In recognition of our financial resources and the location of our physical assets, the organization is able to accept retention of uninsured losses as follows:

- Not more than $_____ arising out of a single event or occurrence.
- Not more than $_____ aggregate during any fiscal year.

Deductibles of less than $_____ will be purchased only when dictated by:

- Cost/benefit comparisons.
- Legal or contractual requirements.
- Desirable insurance carrier services.

g. It will be the responsibility of _____ to manage our insurance and risk management program in accord with this policy statement.

Loss Control Policy Statement

It is the policy of this organization to provide our visitors, employees, and members of the general public with a safe and secure environment.

It is also our policy to protect the physical assets of the organization from fortuitous loss.

To accomplish these two objectives, we will take whatever steps are appropriate to identify sources of loss and then to control losses through a loss control program.

It will be the responsibility of _____ to supervise our loss control program and monitor adherence to this policy.

Risk Management Department

Insert names, telephone numbers (office and home) of key personnel to be contacted for further information or in an emergency.

Outside Vendors

Insert names, addresses, telephone numbers, and functions of outside vendors such as brokers, consultants, and service companies.

Emergency Telephone Numbers

Police, fire, hospital, and the like.

Corporate Indemnification

Describe corporate indemnification of officers, directors and employees.

Uninsured Exposures

Provide schedule of major uninsured exposured.

SECTION III

Claims

Losses must be reported promptly. Late reports may jeopardize claim settlement or abrogate our right to reimbursement. The method and forms used to process a claim vary with the type of claim.

In the absence of any specific claim form, you may use the format indicated below to report a loss as soon as practicable after the loss has been discovered. Furnish as complete and accurate information as is available so that at least a preliminary report may be made to our insurance carrier.

Serious losses should be reported immediately by telephone, teletype, or telegram.

Information to be reported
   a. Date of occurrence: _____
   b. Time: _____
   c. Exact location:_____
   d. Cause of loss: _____
   e. Describe damage: _____
   f. $ Estimate: _____
   g. For additional information contact — Name: _____
                                              Title: _____
                                              Address: _____
                                              Telephone No: _____
   h. This information reported by   — Name: _____
                                              Title: _____
                                              Address: _____
                                              Telephone No: _____
   i. Today's date: _____

SECTION VI

New Exposures
It is extremely important that we be kept aware of new exposures arising as a result of such things as new products, mergers, acquisitions, contracts and leases, new construction, and so forth. An awareness of exposures arising out of our products or services as well as our operations and those exposures contained within contracts and leases is vital. Please keep us abreast of all new exposures that you are aware of.

Types of Information and Source

a.	Accounting	—	Sales, earnings, expenses Cost of raw materials Insurable values Taxes Payrolls
b.	Advertising	—	Advertising copy
c.	Distribution	—	Shipments (outgoing and incoming) Vehicles
d.	Finance	—	Cash flow projections Cost of capital Liquidity Credit
e.	Legal	—	Contracts Leases Agreements Hold-harmless agreements
f.	Personnel	—	New job specifications Pre-employment physicals

		—	EEOA problems
g.	Production	—	Quality control matters Changes in layout New processes Changes in power or water supply
h.	Purchasing	—	Purchase orders Large purchases Lease of equipment
i.	Real Estate	—	New property Leases Construction Watercraft/aircraft
j.	Research and Development	—	New products/services
k.	Sales	—	Sales presentations Territorial changes Changes in distribution Lines of credit Collections

New Construction

It is in our interest to have all plans for new construction reviewed prior to commencing work. This review is primarily designed to ensure that loss prevention is included in the planning phase rather than the more costly expedient of adding protection after construction.

The inclusion of loss prevention devices customarily serves to reduce our insurance premium costs.

Inspections

Insurers and other consultants will make periodic inspection visits to all locations and submit written reports with recommendations for improved loss control. We should cooperate fully with these representatives and will implement all feasible recommendations.

Surety Bonds

Surety bonds are contracts under which the Surety (insurance company) guarantees the fulfillment of an obligation on the part of the Principal (ourselves) to a third party called the Obligee (such as a state or municipal government). The surety bond serves in lieu of collateral. It is not insurance in the pure sense but more akin to a credit relationship.

Bid bonds, contract bonds, and performance bonds are all examples of surety bonds. When requesting a surety bond, please advise us of the following:

- Exact name of obligee.
- Dollar amount of bond.
- Effective date.
- Type of bond. Supply a blank bond form. If one is not available, describe the obligation which is to be guaranteed.

Contractors
In the course of contracting for any construction or service activities, we should require certificates of insurance from contractors and subcontractors evidencing the presence of workers' compensation insurance to meet their statutory obligations as well as public liability and in some cases automobile liability insurance. Liability limits of at least $_____ per person and $_____ per accident for personal injury and $_____ property damage liability are suggested as absolute minimums. Higher limits may be advisable depending upon the character of the project or service.

The contract itself should include a hold harmless clause under which the contractor agrees to indemnify and hold us harmless for accidents arising out of the contractor's (or subcontractor's) negligence.

Requests for Certificate of Insurance
From time to time, we will be requested to supply certificates of insurance to others. These requests will be honored where appropriate. The certificate of insurance will indicate our insurance company, policy number, limits, and expiration date.

Hold Harmless Agreements
Hold harmless agreements may be included in contracts. The effect of a hold harmless agreement may be that we assume unreasonable contractual liabilities. We are fully prepared to cary out our legal responsibilities but some hold harmless and indemnification agreements go far beyond reasonableness in that they relieve the other party from their own negligence.

All requests for hold harmless and indemnification agreements should be submitted to _____ for review prior to signing.

Leases
As a lessor of property, we may be asked to waive subrogation which means that our insurer cannot look to our lessee to collect for a loss paid to us. Similarly, if we are a lessee of property insured by lessor, we should request that the lessor waive subrogation either within the framework of the lease or by separate letter.

Under most circumstances, a mutual waiver of subrogation for losses otherwise covered by insurance between lessor and lessee is a desirable component of lease agreements.

SECTION VII

Reporting of Values
Detail your procedures.

Audits
Discuss audit procedures.

Allocations
Outline your organization's cost-allocation process.

Personal Property of Employees
Company policy and responsibility for personal property (including tools) of employees.

Employee Use of Company Owned/Leased Automobiles
Your policy on this sensitive subject.

Rented Automobiles
Attitude on insurance, deductibles, and the like on rent-a-cars.

Employee Use of Aircraft and Watercraft
Company policy on employee owned or chartered planes and boats.

Key Executives in Single Aircraft
Policy.

Product Recall
Procedures.

Household Goods in Transit
Insurance and responsibility.

Kidnap and Ransom
Policy and procedures.

Travel in War-Risk Zones
Notification, insurance, protection, and the like.

Other
Other company statements on sensitive risk areas.

SECTION VIII

Insurance Policy Description
Insured:

Section: VIII
Page:

Broker:
Property/exposure covered:

Date page issued:

Insurance Carrier:
Policy Period:

Policy No:
Premium: $
Payment method:

Peris insured:
Amount/limits of coverage:
Retentions:
Significant exclusions:

Territory:
Valuation:
Other interests:

Claims instructions:

Significant endorsements:

Special terms and conditions such as cancellation, reports, notice and proof of loss, inspection, subrogation, duties of insured, and key definitions:

2.1.5 The risk management report

Most firms produce a range of in-house reports during any one year. There are reports on research and development, marketing, new products, advertising, changes in the organisation, acquisitions and mergets etc., etc. The annual risk management report would simply be one of these reports. It would be produced and distributed once a year and would cover a whole range of risk management related problems.

There is a wide diversity as to style, and indeed use of such reports, and so it is not possible to say that there is one single style which is the preferred one. Each organisation has to produce reports which fit in with the general image of the company as a whole and the risk manager's report must fit into this mould as well as any other manager's.

What we have produced are three different contents pages which give some idea of the possible contents of a report. These samples are shown in Fig 2.6.

Fig 2.6

(A)
RISK MANAGEMENT REPORT

- Summary
- Highlights of the year
- Loss Analysis
  - Insurance claims
  - Uninsured losses
- Premiums paid
- Inter-Group Comparisons
  —
- Conclusions

(B)
RISK MANAGEMENT REPORT

- The Risk Management Department
- Corporate Risk Management Philosophy
- Implementing the philosophy
- Review of loss producing events

- Risk Financing analysis
- Five year comparisons
- The next five years
- Summary of major points

(C)
RISK MANAGEMENT REPORT

- Introduction
- Property Risks
- Pecuniary Risks
- Liability Risks
- Transport Risks
- Major Incidents Summary
- Expected Changes
- Conclusions

These three report formats are really quite different. Style (a) seems to concentrate on the insured/uninsured distinction while style (b) features the philosophy and has more general divisions. Sample (c) has used the type of risk itself as a means of structuring the report. You can see that the same information could easily be contained in each one of these reports, it is just a matter of judgement as to which one suits the orgnisation best.

What value could we say that these reports have?

- They do represent excellent public relations. It is an opportunity for the risk manager to put foward a "good" image of his function and the work of his department. So much of the year will have been spent dealing with people when they have had some loss or other traumatic experience. It is good to be able to put forward a slightly different image at least once a year.

- The very discipline of having to carry out the work necessary in the preparation of the report may well reveal information which may otherwise have been hidden. Preparing the report will take some time, if it is to be done properly, and it may well be that the work proves to be of value in itself

- The annual report can act as a good educational tool for the risk manager. We have mentioned several times that the essence of risk management often lies in communicating the message of risk. The report gives the risk manager the opportunity to put over some ideas in a manner and in a document which stands a chance of being read.

- The report can also be quite reassuring to other managers in the company. It is very easy, once you have had a loss, to think that you are the only person or division sustaining a loss like this. The risk manager has the overall view and is able to report on the whole range of losses sustained within the company. Reading these loss reports may well let some managers see that they are not as bad as they thought they were. The opposite can also be the case, where a manager has been complaining that his record is not as bad as the premiums indicate. If indeed he has had a bad record then this will be reflected in the figures for his department or division.

So far then we have dealt with the role of the risk manager as a policy maker. The issues we have raised are all of a strategic nature and involve the risk manager in the laying down of the general thrust of the risk management philosophy. We will turn now to look at the department itself and the work it will do.

2.2   The Risk Management Department

The distinction between the risk manager and the risk management department will seem kind of academic to many. In practice most risk managers work in very small departments where they cannot afford the luxury of a policy maker and a department to carry out the policy. Creating the distinction was, however, a tool to help in our understanding of the different roles which have to be performed. Once we have a measure of all the tasks which have to be done we can then relate it to our own circumstances. Remember that the Diploma is intended to educate in the area of risk management, not to train you for any one specific function. The success or otherwise of a course lies in your ability to apply what you have studied to practical situations as and when appropriate.

Let us leave the risk manager then, and turn to the work of the department itself. Under the control and guidance of the risk manager, exactly what is its function?

2.2.1   Identification of loss

One of the essential and most time consuming roles of the department is in the identification of loss. The department will be involved in creating and using the correct methodology for the identification of risk in the company. This will mean using existing techniques and adapting others for use by the company. It will also mean keeping accurate records of all site visits and other risk identification methods. For example, if the company makes use of Hazard and Operability Studies then these will have to be carefully logged and updated when required. The same is the case for fault trees, check lists, flow charts and other techniques.

2.2.2 Implementing risk control philosophy

The department will have the responsibility of keeping up to date on all the operations within the company and of ensuring that the risk control measures which have been decided upon are in fact implemented. There are two quite distinct tasks involved here. First the risk management department has to be aware or make itself aware of all the new developments in the company and second, must attempt to implement the risk control measures which it sees as most appropriate for the new development.

Linked to this is the continual need to be abreast of new developments in the field of risk control. For many risk managers this may also mean keeping up to date on safety technology as well as on physical risk control methods.

2.2.3 Keep accurate records

An important feature of any department's work is keeping records. These records have to be accurate and accessible, they must be held in such a way as they can be updated easily. The risk manager has any number of different types of records and today the computer is a great help both in storing information and in retrieving it.

The kind of information a risk manager has on record could include:

- **loss records**
- **actual losses**
- **near misses**
- **costs of losses**
- **reserves etc.**
- **details of insurance premiums**
- **payroll figures**
- **staff numbers**
- **acquisitions and mergers**
- **all risk identification records**
- **safety documents.**

2.2.4 Insurance management

Insurance is still a major function in most risk management departments and while it is still only an aspect of risk management itself, it does occupy a great deal of the time of the risk manager. Managing the insurance portfolio for a large concern is almost a job in its own right. It will involve:

- assessing the need for covers of different types
- selecting insurers and brokers

- evaluating premiums
- matching and dovetailing of covers
- negotiating on price
- drafting wordings
- dealing with claims
- keeping all insurance records

This is clearly not a comprehensive list, and many readers will be able to expand on it from their own experience. It is however large enough to show the magnitude of the task and the work entailed in managing a large insurance portfolio.

2.2.5 Attending to all other aspects of the risk management philosophy

This last point is a kind of "catch all" for all the hundreds of jobs which are not capable of being defined under a neat heading. It would include, for example, training of staff in the department, regular meetings on risk and safety matters with other managers, seminars for senior staff. Under this heading we might also consider the training of new entrants to the organisation, particularly new graduate entrants. Those who enter the company as graduate trainees will normally be spoken to by a number of line managers during their *induction* and there is no reason why the risk manager should not be included. A less attractive feature of "Attending to all other aspects . . ." will of course include responding to the constant run of telephone enquiries and acting as a general "Aunt Sally" when required.

2.3 Location and Structure of the Risk Management Department

We have now looked at the duties of the risk manager and of the risk management department, recognising that these may well be carried out by the same person in many organisations. What we must do now is to look at the risk management department itself, in the context of the structure of the company as a whole. The risk management department is simply one of the departments in the organisation and like all others it will have its own structure and its own positioning within the company framework. In this final section we will spend some time looking at the structure which a risk managsement department may take and at its location within the organisation.

2.3.1 Structure

There can be no model for the structure of a risk management department as the exact structure will depend entirely on the organisation itself. There are risk management departments ranging from one person to over sixty people and so it does not make sense to suggest that one model structure can be created.

What might be useful would be to take a look at a number of different structures which could apply, depending on the size of the department. Two possible structures are shown in Fig 2.7.

Fig 2.7(a)

Fig 2.7(b)

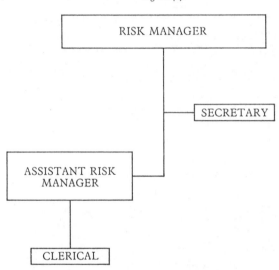

The structure in Fig 2.7(a) is of the department which is staffed by one person on their own. There is one person performing the risk management function and a secretary to assist. The second structure in Fig 2.7 has two people and some administrative assistance. In structures like this we are not necessarily thinking of small firms. There can be some quite large companies which prefer to organise their central services, like risk management, in this way. They will have a small department and will possibly contract out a lot of the work which would otherwise have been handled by staff in-house. For example the insurance work may well be handled by a broker, the safety work by some consultancy and loss control bought in as a service. This has its advantages and disadvantages but clearly a philosophy like this has the result that the in-house risk management function need only be very small.

27

The structures in Fig 2.8 are a little different.

Fig 2.8(a)

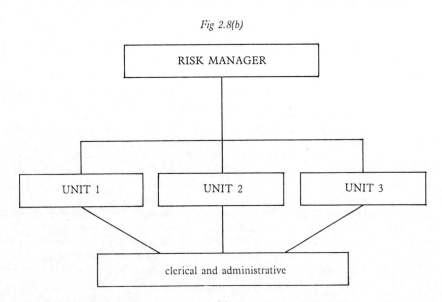

Fig 2.8(b)

In Fig 2.8(a) we see a structure which has separated the insurance function from the safety function. This is simply by way of example. We could equally well have had the loss control function separate from the safety function or security out on its own. The main point to grasp is that it is possible to identify certain main aspects of risk management and have them as units within the department as a whole. The advantage of doing this is probably that it allows for a greater level of accountability if units are now visible within the entire structure. The risk manager can set targets for each unit and can monitor the progress in each case a little more easily than if the various functions were all together. The main disadvantage is that it is a bit heavy on the paper work and administration required.

In our illustration we have split the safety and insurance functions. This seems a fairly obvious split and it means that the different people can get on with their particular job. Each unit would have its own clerical assistance and would of course report back through the risk manager.

In Fig 2.8(b) we have shown a structure which is split according to a number of units. These units could be any suitable division within the company. It may be that the company already splits into geographical units for administrative reasons. If this is the case then it does seem logical that the risk management department adopt the same split. Remember that a great deal of data flows into risk management department from the various operating units of the company and the risk manager must make it as easy for this data to flow as possible. At the very least he should avoid creating administrative barriers or hurdles over which the operating managers have to jump. If the company is split according to area of the country, countries of the world or products, the risk manager would be wise to consider splitting his own department in the same way. It does take time to work out what the best structure might be, but it will pay dividends in the end.

2.3.2   Location

We have said already that the best risk management statement in the world and the most perfect philosophy will be ineffective if they are not implemented. The actual location of the risk management department can go a long way to assisting in the implementation of policy. If the department is situated at a reasonably high level in the organisation and the risk manager reports at a high level then the whole function will be seen as having some *clout*. This implied authority may well assist the risk manager from time to time.

In the 1983 AIRMIC survey of the status of its members, they were asked how and to whom they reported:

    50.7% reported at main board leval
    38.0% reported through the company secretary
    13.2% reported through a financial manager/director
    13.6% reported to the managing director.

This does tend to support the contention that most departments report at a high level. In the main reporting is carried out through a financial executive rather than, for example, a production director. Anyone who has spent even a short period in industry knows how important the finance function is, and those who control it. In the end, risk management is only one more tool to help the company achieve its profit goal and so its costs and benefits in monetary terms are important.

2.4   Conclusion

The emphasis in this chapter has been on the broader, managerial or corporate aspects of risk management. The risk manager cannot forget that he is a manager and is therefore subject to all the criteria by which other managers are normally judged. The discipline of risk management has its technical aspects, in the same way as all other management disciplines have their own body of techniques, but in the end the risk manager must manage.

This chapter has introduced the idea that a risk management philosophy, and the publishing of that philosophy, is an essential part of the risk manager's job. Providing information by means of a manual is also valuable as is the regular issue of risk management reports. This all relates to the relationship which the risk manager hopes to have or to build with those around him in the organisation. He also has responsibilities to those within his own department and must look to their individual needs, as their superior.

The whole business of risk management is very much a *people* business. Relationships, the ability to create them and sustain them, are of the essence in effective risk management and the art of building these relationships is not learned from text books. Experience is what teaches one how to respond to different people inside and outside the organisation.

In the chapters which follow we turn to a number of specific management issues, the most important one of which is the whole business of making decisions. After looking at decision making we move on to business forecasting before picking up the two specific areas of international risk management and disaster planning.

Chapter 3

RISK MANAGEMENT DECISIONS

3.0 The whole process of management is concerned with decision making. Any business relies on effective decision making for its very survival and the history of British industry is chequered with the effects of bad decisions.

The task of decision making is probably the most important role performed by any manager. Some management scholars have argued that management *is* decision making and everything a manager does he does through decision making. These decisions range from relatively simple decisions through to complex questions of product design, location of plant, marketing options and so on.

The risk manager is in exactly the same position as any other manager as far as the importance of decision making is concerned. He is confronted with a bewildering array of decision situations and his survival and hence the well-being of the organisation rests on him being able to take the best course of action. For the risk manager the task of decision making is very much the bottom line of his function. After risks have been identified and analysis carried out, comes the decision; After reviewing loss records and looking at trends, comes the decision; After seeking renewal terms, looking over terms and conditions, comes the decision.

The range of risk management decisions is vast, including decisions in areas such as:

- insurance covers
- deductibles
- choice of insurers
- retention levels
- alternative risk financing mechanisms
- control mechanisms
- use of brokers
- captive formation
- choice of reinsurers
  etc., etc.

We can add to this the whole range of general management type decisions such as those provided in the field of personnel, planning, policy making, budgeting etc. Gradually a picture emerges of an almost constant round of decision making, either consciously carried out or not.

It is as well then that we spend some time looking at decision making. It is appropriate that any study of decision making comes towards the end of the syllabus as only then will the reader have assimilated all the other skills and knowledge necessary for the taking of decisions.

In this chapter we will concentrate on the process by which decisions are made, looking at the qualitative aspects of decision making, covering topics such as recognising and defining decision problems, decision objectives and the structure of decisions. Chapters four and five turn to the more quantitative aspects of decision analysis.

3.1 Decision Making

Several times we have used the phrases "decision making" and "decision taking". It may be useful to distinguish between these phrases for the purposes of our study. We would be best to look upon decision making in the sense of decision building or decision constructing and then we can leave the term decision taking to describe the final act of selecting one course of action. This may seem a rather theoretical and needless distinction but it does help to concentrate the mind on the building of the various components of a decision.

Distinguishing between building a decision and taking a decision also underlines the important fact that decision making "per se" is important. In fact, we could say that the process by which we make decisions assumes an importance which is quite distinct from the detail of any one decision.

There are many models, or ways of displaying the decision process. One illustration is shown in Fig 3.1.

Fig 3.1

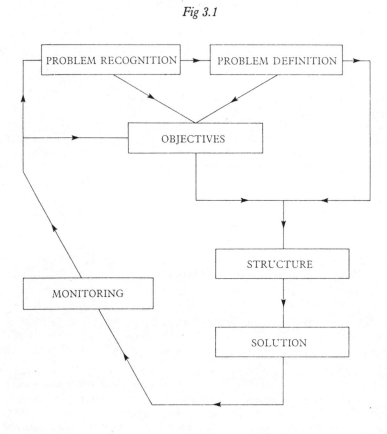

RISK MANAGEMENT DECISIONS

In this illustration we can see a number of distinct stages in the decision process. We will follow each stage through in this chapter and the next.

The illustration shows the emphasis on building up the various components of the decision, before the final step of actually taking one course of action as opposed to the other. It is valuable to get clear in our mind at this early stage that the only reason we have a decision problem is because there is more than one course of action open to us.

Any decision implies a choice. If there is only one possible action open to us then there is no decision problem. We can think of this even in relation to our private domestic situation before looking at business decision problems. Let us say you want to make a trip to some other city, Paris for example. A number of options immediately present themselves. You have a choice of mode of transport, who to go with, time of day, time of year and so on. Each of these choices also raise another sub-set of problems. Think of the mode of transport. How many different ways of getting to Paris are there? You could go by train and boat, bus and boat, plane, bicycle, hitch-hike, ...! Each one of these options is perfectly feasible but in selecting one you will have in mind considerations such as cost, length of journey, comfort of the journey, reliability, safety, etc. You may want to fly but also want the cheapest way of travel. You may prefer the bus but want to get there as soon as possible. What we have is a fairly complex problem and somehow a decision has to be taken. We may not be conscious of going through any kind of decision process but somehow all these various inputs and pieces of information have to be received, processed and finally one option selected as the preferred mode.

The same process goes on continually; where will we eat, what will we wear, where will we live, what kind of career to follow, what car to buy, which house to purchase and so on. We cannot escape the need to make and take decisions. Fortunately the built-in computer each of us carries in our head, is capable of processing complex situations and of leading us to one option as opposed to another.

In our business life the decisions become more and more complex; what machine to buy, where to site a factory, should we diversify or not etc.

Each one of these decisions raises hundreds of other issues. Which machine to buy leads into considering the cost, the availability, reliability, efficiency, ease of use, output, view of the relevant union and so on. Each one of these sub-issues raises other problems and so it goes on. The decision becomes a complex mass of inform-ation with innumerable inputs and conflicts. At the end, however, judgement will have to be exercised and a choice made.

We may be able to cope with most domestic decision problems without having to fall back on any formal tools to help but the same cannot be said of business decisions. The complexity of most business decisions is such that we do need some guide to handling them, some method, a formal approach.

We can begin to see the essence of such an approach in the way we have already begun to dissect problems into various parts. The trip to Paris, the purchase of machinery were each broken down to reveal other, hidden aspects of the decision. The key to the successful analysis of decisions does seem to be in the decomposition of problems. If we can break a problem down into its component parts then we can begin to look at each part in detail before re-assembling the bits to lead us towards a final choice.

This idea is not new, nor is it in any sense novel or original to this course. There are very many text books dealing with management decision making and almost all of them start from the premise that decisions have to be broken down. This "divide to conquer" rule is seen clearly in the decision process model illustrated in Fig 3.1. We will take each part in turn and in fact further reduce each part, all with the aim of helping us to make, and actually take, better decisions.

3.2   Preparing for Decision Making

The very beginning of the decision making process is the recognition that a decision has to be taken.

3.2.1   Problem Recognition

Realising that a decision is required is the first step. It is obvious that the best decision can only be taken at the end of the day if it was firstly recognised in the beginning. What we are really saying is that the need to make a decision was seen, that an unsatisfactory state was recognised. Some writers would say that what we need to do is to recognise that a state of dis-equilibrium exists. This may seem a very "fancy" way of saying that all is not well and that something has to be done or decided.

This recognition that some decision is called for can be stimulated by internal or external factors. Literally, the risk manager himself may recognise the need for some action. Some review of work practices, loss records, policy wordings etc., may highlight points which would form the basis of the need for a decision.

In many instances, however, the stimulus to think about decisions or even to recognise that a decision is required, comes from some external source. Examples of such an external influence could include:

● the report of some committee. It may well be that you receive the report from a safety committee, planning group, finance committee or the like, and from that report find that there is the need to make a decision. The findings of a committee may ask you to make a decision, this is the simplest case, or more likely may highlight a problem which requires examination.

● there may be some sudden change, some dramatic event which necessitates a decision. A major fire, loss of life, collapse of insurer, political upheaval etc., could all act as a stimulus to recognise the need to make a decision.

● you may receive some instruction from a higher authority which asks you to make a decision. The finance director may write saying he would like you to consider a change of broker, forming a captive, cancelling some covers.

If we think back to our simple, domestic decision problem concerned with the trip to Paris then we can see that the recognition of the need to make that decision could have been generated:

● Internally   — we may simply have wanted a holiday or a change of scene for some other reason, and decided on Paris.

34

● Externally   — we may have been invited for a job interview or have been asked to visit Paris by an employer or to gain some other work experience.

It is exactly the same in risk management decisions we have the:

● Internal stimulus   — Surveys
                         — loss records
                         — policy reviews
                         — site visits
                         — renewal seasons
                         — safety audits
                         etc.

and we have:

● External stimulus   — large losses
                         — instructions from superiors
                         — acquisitions and mergers
                         — financial or environmental changes
                         — legal or political influences
                         — social changes.

Once we have recognised the need for a decision it is essential that we do not rush into solving the decision problem. Firstly, we should spend some time making sure we understand the nature of the problem we have identified.

3.2.2 Problem Definition

This important stage of defining the decision problem is often overlooked in the rush to take the decision and to select the one course of action. Often a solution is adopted simply in order to move on to the next problem and in retrospect it proves to be a less than optimum decision.

There are some guidelines we could have in mind when thinking about defining the nature of the decision.

(a) We should try to frame a clear problem statement. The solution, whatever it will be, will only be as good as the definition of our problem. An ill-defined problem will inevitably lead to a poor decision.

We should ensure that what we state as our decision problem, is really the problem and not simply the symptom. We may have been reviewing our employee injury records and recognised a large number of back injuries. Having recognised this we should look at it a little more closely and see what the problem really is. It is unlikely that the problem is back injuries, this is probably the symptom, the real problem may be the system of work, positioning of machines, weight of objects and so on. This may then lead us down several other paths which, if we had limited our problem definition to back injuries, may have remained hidden from us.

(b) We should try to avoid implied solutions. We all have a fairly strong tendency to think about problems in terms of their solution. In doing this we can unconsciously jump over a number of other very acceptable solutions in the rush to get to our own.

For example we may have identified an employee who has been involved in a number of small accidents on the shop floor. Recognising this as a problem and seeing that there is the need to make some decision, it would be very easy to jump straight to a solution. We might state the problem as being, "How to make the process in which this man is involved, safer".

This definition of the problem in terms of the implied solution then overlooks a wider range of possible solutions such as moving the man, re-training him, alerting his foreman etc.

Framing our problem statement in the form of an implied solution, in this way, often arises because managers *learn* experiences rather than learn from them. They think back to some previous problem they had and try to apply solutions which have failed in the past!

(c) We should consult those around us. It may well be that aspects of the decision problem lie hidden from you for whatever reason. If this is the case then there will be merit in consulting other people in the organisation.

It is certainly not a sign of inadequacy or defeat if you have to speak to a few other managers and get their views on whatever decision problem you are defining.

(d) Try to look at the problem from a wide angle. Risk managers should be particularly good at this. They should be used to looking at issues without blinkers and including inputs from a range of disciplines.

It is the same with decisions and especially defining decision problems. It is useful to leave a problem for a day or overnight and come back to it afresh. It is surprising how often one generates new thoughts after reflecting on a problem for a while.

(e) The time scale within which events are to happen must also be taken into account. A temporary water shortage should not lead us to define our problem in terms of building our own reservoir. The closure of a local reservoir may well however, lead us to define our problem in terms of finding a new long term source of water for say, our sprinkler installation.

3.2.3 Processing Information

So far we have looked at the need to recognise that a decision has to be made and at the necessity of defining the decision problem. Before going on to look at further aspects or components of a decision let us take a little time to explore further the way in which we as individuals process information.

We said earlier that even the simplest of decisions involves a whole range of different factors, all of which have to be processed in such a way as to produce a final selection or judgement. How the brain actually copes with all of this information and refines it for us is not all that well understood. What might be beneficial for our study is to look at the consequences of being human and hence of only having limited capabilities as far as processing information is concerned. If we are alert to these facts, or even simply aware of them, then it may aid our decision making process.

(a) The first consequence of our limited processing capacity is that we tend to be selective in the information we retain. When we are confronted, or more often bombarded, with a great volume of information we do tend to select only part of it. We do this often on the basis of familiarity or seeing what you anticipated seeing.

Selecting information on the basis of familiarity can be tested with a trick pack of cards. If you produce one playing card which is in fact a *red* spade e.g., a red three of spades. Clearly such a card does not exist but if you show a number of ordinary cards to people, with the trick card in the middle and ask them to write down quickly what they see you get interesting results. Very many people simply write down for the trick card that they saw the three of spades or the three of hearts. They were selecting information on the basis of images with which they were familiar.

Risk managers can surely fall into the same trap, looking at a contract and relating it incorrectly to a similar wording seen before. Looking for things you expect to see was the other reason for selective processing of information and we are all guilty of doing this from time to time. Charles Osgood, in his book, "Method and Theory in Experimental Research" discusses this point in relation to visual images. He suggests that once you are told what a drawing represents it is very difficult to see anything else in it. For example, look at the drawings in Fig 3.2 and decide what the picture is telling you.

Fig 3.2(a)   *Fig 3.2(b)*

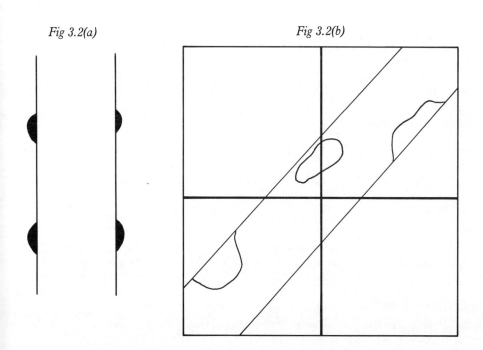

Now, you are told that the first picture 3.2(a) is a bear climbing a tree and the second 3.2(b) is a giraffe passing a window. Look away from the pictures for a short time. When you look back it is just exceptionally difficult *not* to see the bear or the giraffe.

It is exactly the same with our decision information processing. You are reading the facts of a complicated decision and all the time you select pieces of information depending upon whether certain facts are more familiar than others and also whether they match your expectations.

(b) The second consequence of having limited information processing capabilities is that we end up processing the information in some kind of time order. It is clearly impossible for us to deal with all the information simultaneously and so some ordering is inevitable. We can recognise this in many ordinary decisions, walking along the road we take one decision after another, go left, cross the road, wait at the kerb, go right etc.

This is fine for decisions where action in the short term is required and short term results are expected. For many decisions however we work on far longer time scales and sequential processing of information becomes much harder. The decision as to the retention level of a captive, purchase of new safety guards etc., are decisions with relatively long term consequences. Our limited processing capability may well lead to our not considering all the longer term aspects of the decision.

(c) Another consequence of limited processing capacity is that we may well only recall information from our memory in a selective way. The computer will memorise any information you give it and will recall it at command. Our human memory is not as reliable, we can all testify to that I am sure.

In a decision making context we may well find ourselves recalling only partial information rather than all the facts we once had.

We usually end up using some kind of help or cue to assist us in recalling data. One thing we often do is to reconstruct data according to some base or anchoring point. For example, look at the two sets of letters below, for a second only:

(a)

R U N T H E R I S K

(b)

K U T E R I R N S H

Without looking back at the two sets can you now write them down in exactly the same way? It is obvious what is happening, most people will get (a) as it reads out in an easily recognisable form i.e., Run the Risk. The second is much more difficult to reconstruct and most people will not get past the first few letters.

In a decision making sense the same can happen. We can see facts and later reconstruct them in some way and then depending on how easy the facts are to recall, we will do a good or bad job.

Given these and other problems it is essential that we very carefully structure our decision making to minimise the chances of us falling into these traps and pitfalls.

3.3 Decision Objectives

Once the need to make a decision has been recognised and the problem defined we are almost ready to move on to the judgement stage. There is one final step which is essential. We must work out what the objectives of our decision are. In other words we must work out why we are deciding anything at all. If we have no notion of what it is we hope to achieve then there is no hope of us being able to say whether or not we have achieved it.

3.3.1 Objective or Objectives

Achieving the ideal position in any decision making situation is probably not possible. What we can strive for is to satisfy a number of lesser criteria. This is a useful way to think of objectives. There is some goal which is almost unattainable and objectives measure how far we have moved along the road towards the goal. In a domestic sense we may have a goal or ideal of securing "happiness". The chances of securing complete happiness are probably not all that high and so you may settle for some lesser goal of being as happy as you can.

A company may have a goal of eliminating pollution or having no employee injuries, but it may have to settle for minimising pollution and reducing injuries.

Rarely, however, will there be one single objective. Being as happy as you can may be achieveable in a number of different ways, for example,

- by increasing our income
- by enjoying our work
- by being married
- by having children etc., etc.

In the same way we will find that business decisions will have several objectives. Minimising the output of noxious fumes may also be considered with maintaining production levels, reducing fuel costs and so on.

3.3.2 Conflict among Objectives

The fact that any one decision can have multiple objectives leads to the inevitable position where one objective is in conflict with others. In our simple domestic example of being happy we had objectives of increasing your income and enjoying your work. There may be no conflict between these two objectives and in such a case we could aim to satisfy both. For many people, however, increasing your income may mean doing an unpleasant job or working unusual hours and so you may not meet the objective of enjoying your work while satisfying the objective of maximising your income.

In the pollution example we can also see this conflict. Reducing the emission of noxious fumes may conflict with using the most economic fuel and reducing fuel costs may not be attainable at current levels of production. There is a classic conflict situation and moreover it may well be that in attaining one objective you actually lower or eliminate the chance of securing others.

This dilemma is often referred to as sub-optimisation and can arise in at least two ways.

(a) Internal sub-optimisation. Where the conflict arises solely due to the objectives set by the risk manager himself or those laid down in some philosophy or policy statement, we could say that we have internal sub-optimisation.

Take the example of the risk manager who may set objectives for his insurance programme which include:

- achieve the most favourable wording
- maximise the deductible discount
- buy from the British market.

In such a case there are a number of sub-optimisations problems:

- the best wording may not be British
- the best discount may have the worst wording
- the best discount may not be British.

(b) External sub-optimisation. Let us consider an example where the risk manager has an objective such as, "to protect employees from machine injury".

There may well be others in the organisation who have formed objectives which will prove to be sub-optimal with the risk manager's objective. For example the production manager may want to "maximise output". Finance may want to "minimise production costs and capital expenditure" and marketing may want to be "first in the market place with the new product".

Clearly there will be sub-optimisation if the risk manager wants to fit a new style of guard, in order to satisfy his objectives but finds that the guard causes a reduction in output levels and is very expensive.

It is quite easy to raise this problem of sub-optimisation and to give examples. It is much more difficult to suggest how it should be tackled.

3.4   Structure of Decisions

Before moving on to look at the analysis of decisions, the task of actually taking the decision, there is one final feature of decisions we should get clear. A decision, and we are concerned primarily with decisions under uncertain conditions, has a structure. Let us think of a simple everyday decision in order to illustrate this point.

Think for a moment about the decision you take every day at lunch time as to where you are going to eat. This is a fairly simple decision and most of us will give very little conscious thought to it.

Let us see if we can work out some kind of decision protocol or thinking process which a person goes through, albeit subjectively.

- First   — We assume that we are going to eat. In terms of our earlier model of the decision process we have recognised a decision problem and defined it. We do this unconsciously, or perhaps our stomachs send a more audible message. However it happens, we recognise the need

40

to make a decision and define the decision in terms of where we are to eat.

● Second — we review all the possible venues open to us. We could use:

    — the staff canteen
    — a nearby restaurant
    — the bar across the road
    — a fast food joint round the corner
    — or indeed we could eat something at our desk.

● Third — we may have certain objectives in mind which we want to satisfy. For example we may:

    — want to minimise cost
    — eat quality food
    — have a very quick lunch
    — not want to be far from the office.

We can see right away the old problem of sub-optimisation. How can we eat quality food while minimising the cost? Can we have a quick lunch while not being far from the office etc., etc.?

● Fourth — You know what you like. You have some idea of what you are looking for and will have some way of judging when you are satisfied. It may be difficult for us to describe this part of the process, a priori, but after the event we will be able to say if we were satisfied with the meal or not.

● Fifth — You make some judgement as to where you are going to eat. You can't wait too long before deciding, or sleep on the idea, or delay the decision for a few days if it is 11.00 a.m. The decision has to be taken fairly quickly.

This whole process is the "making" of the decision. We have assembled the component parts. In fact, in a simple decision such as this the process is undertaken almost simultaneously and the decision taken at the end. But for our purposes it is useful to tease out the various strands of the decision making process.

What seems to have happened is that:

● a problem was recognised and defined
● objectives were established
● alternative courses of action were listed
● a means of measuring satisfaction was sought
● finally a judgement was taken.

So far in this chapter we have looked at the question of recognising problems, defining problems and setting objectives. What we have not yet looked at are the final three stages of listing alternatives, measuring satisfaction and actually taking the decision.

This then is the classic structure of decisions. We have alternatives and look for some measurement of how effective each pay-off is and then we take the decision.

We could have two machines x and y. The production rate from machine x is 500 units an hour and from y is 700 per hour. The alternatives are either x or y and the way we are measuring the value of each alternative is by comparing the units processed per hour. The units processed is our pay-off measure, it is our way of judging how satisfied we will be with each machine. What we have therefore is a simple structure:

Alternatives	Pay-offs
x	500
y	700

If we had no other factors to consider then we would probably decide on y because of its higher pay-off.

In risk management terms we could have three quotations for a particular form of insurance cover:

Alternatives	Pay-offs (Premiums)
Insurer A	£10,000
Insurer B	£12,000
Insurer C	£8,000

Again, if all other factors were the same then we would decide on the Insurer C.

Both of these examples are far too simple but they do illustrate the basic structure of a problem. In the real world we would have a fairly complicated process to go through before reaching a final pay-off. In the case of the machines we would, in addition to production rates, want to consider the initial cost, depreciation, maintenance, reliability, cost of running them etc., etc.

3.4.1   Uncertainty

There is one other way in which these two examples are unrealistic. They both make no mention of uncertainty. Most business decisions are not taken in an atmosphere of total certainty. Even in the case of the purchase of machine x or y we may make some estimate of the production rate of each machine but we do not know for sure how efficient each one will be until we have used them.

We have to be clear that what we mean by uncertainty is not that the alternatives or pay-offs are uncertain but that the whole decision is taken in an uncertain environment.

Say you have an amount of money to invest, £1000. You list a number of alternatives for such an investment and measure their effectiveness in terms of the return at the end of one year. Let us limit our alternatives to three, at the moment.

a) Fixed Interest Securities
b) Unit Trust
c) Speculative Shares.

We know that the return on the fixed interest securities is, let us say, 5%. The return on the Unit Trust you have in mind was 7% last year and last year the Shares you intend buying showed a return of 6% over the year.

What we are left with then is a decision which looks like this:

Alternatives	Pay-offs
Fixed Interest Securities	
Unit Trust	
Speculative Shares	

The difficulty is in completing the pay-off column. We could show the figures we have at the moment.

Alternatives	Pay-offs
Fixed Interest Securities	£50
Unit Trust	£70
Speculative Shares	£60

This would lead us to select the Unit Trust assuming we want to maximise return. The problem, of course, is that we do not know what will happen next year. Will the figures of last year be repeated? Will the trust do better or worse? Will share prices increase or decrease?

The return on the fixed Interest Securities is the only thing which is known for sure. The other two alternatives yield outcomes which are uncertain. In simple, general terms we could say that the economy as a whole may stay the same, it may fall or it may rise. If it stays the same our guess is that the returns will be as we have shown above. However, if the economy falls then both the Unit Trust and the Shares will show a lower return. Similarly if the economy rises we would hope that the Unit Trust and the Shares will reflect this. In other words we do not know what will happen and so we cannot say, with certainty, what the pay-offs for each alternative will be.

In fact this is very like a game of chance or indeed a game against the forces of nature. Nature is some mechanism which produces events in the real world, in our example a rising, falling or stable economy. Those who have studied decision making recognised this relationship and coined the term, "States of Nature" to describe the events.

In our example, when we take the three states of nature into account we have a decision structure as follows:

	States of Nature		
Alternatives	Economy Falls	Economy Stable	Economy Rises
Fixed Interest Securities			
Unit Trust			
Speculative Shares			

This decision matrix shows quite clearly that there is one pay-off for each Alternative/State of Nature combination. In this example we end up with nine such combinations. The nature of uncertainty in the decision is that we do not know which one will occur. We know what the alternatives are and what the pay-offs or outcomes are in each case, these are not uncertain. What generates the uncertainty is that we do not know what state of nature will apply. We will see as we go on that this lack of knowledge or imperfection in our knowledge about the future is at the root of most problems in decision analysis. If we had some kind of crystal ball which gave us a certain insight into the future then we would be able to make the best decision.

We can see this if we now complete the decision matrix by including some pay-offs for each alternative/state of nature combination.

Alternatives	States of Nature		
	Economy Falls	Economy Stable	Economy Rises
Fixed Interest Securities	50	50	50
Unit Trust	40	70	100
Speculative Shares	10	60	120

We can see that the return on the fixed interest option remains constant at 5% regardless of what happens in the economy. On the other hand we see that the unit trust could drop to 4% and rise to 10% if the state of the economy changes. The shares show the most dramatic fluctuation as you might expect. The return could be as high as 12% or as low as 1%. If we only knew what was going to happen then we could take the best decision.

If your crystal ball told us that the economy was going to fall, we would take the Fixed Interest Securities as this maximises our return. The Unit Trust would be the best alternative to select if we had certain knowledge that the economy was to remain stable. Finally if we knew for sure that the economy would rise then we would certainly go for the shares, and the high return of 12%.

This then is the very essence of our decision analysis. Which alternative will we select? How will we decide which alternative to choose? How do we cope with the imperfections in our knowledge about the future?

We will hold these questions and the picture of the decision matrix, we have just created, in our mind and in this chapter and the next hope to find some answers.

The matrix we created is a good model for many forms of decisions taken in conditions of uncertainty and indeed we could generalise from the simple interest problem to generate a matrix suitable for all such problems.

	$s1$	$s2$	$s3$ .... sn
$a1$	$o11$	$o12$	$o13$ .... $o1n$
$a2$	$o21$	$o22$	$o23$ .... $o2n$
$a3$	$o31$	$o32$	$o33$ .... $o3n$
•	•	•	• •
•	•	•	• •
•	•	•	• •
am	$om1$	$om2$	$om3$ omn

Where

s = the state of nature ...... up to the nth state

a = the alternative courses of action ...... up to the mth alternative

o = the outcome for each alternative and state of nature combination ...... right up to the outcome corresponding to the mth alternative and nth state of nature

and $o11$ is the outcome for the first alternative/state of nature combination.

This general model can also be used in a risk management situation, for example:

	No loss	Medium loss	Large loss
Full insurance			
Insurance with a deductible			
No insurance			

Here we have a simple three by three decision matrix of our insurance purchasing decision. There are three alternatives and three states of nature. This is clearly far too simplistic to be representative of anything which could happen in the real world. It does however give a more relevant example.

We could use the same basic model to illustrate a loss control type of decision:

	No fire	Device controls fire	Device does not control fire
Smoke Detectors			
Sprinklers			
Fire extinguishers			

We can see once more that we have alternative courses of action. This time they are risk control mechanisms. We have states of nature, in this example, of whether or not there is a fire and if so the efficiency of the device. Finally we have nine alternative/state of nature combinations.

We have used decisions with a three by three form of matrix quite often now. This is not to imply that all decisions involve three alternatives and have three states of nature. The format of decisions is as varied as there are different decisions. The use of the three by three matrix simply allows the essential points to be illustrated with ease. You can imagine that in the real world we may have more or less than three alternatives and will certainly have a large number of states of nature. Fortunately the increasing availability of computer packages, such as electronic spread-sheets, make it relatively simple to construct very large matrices.

In the next chapter we will move on to look at how we will analyse a decision in order to decide which alternative to select. We will conclude this chapter now by taking each part of the structure of our decision matrix in turn. Alternatives, States of nature and Pay-offs and examine them.

3.4.2 Alternatives

There is only a decision if there is at least a choice between alternatives. If there is only one possible course of action open to you then there is no decision. Even where there is only one course of action but you can also decide to do nothing, then there is a choice open to you and hence a decision. It goes without saying, therefore, that the best decision will only be taken at the end of the day if the alternative which will lead to it was included in the list of alternatives in the first place.

The search for all possible relevant alternatives is important. The risk manager may generate alternatives himself or be offered some by others within his company, indeed some may be thrust upon him for example, alternatives generated by some change in law or company policy.

What may be instructive is to look at ways in which the search for alternatives may be limited.

External limitations

We could imagine three main ways in which factors external to the risk manager may place limitations on the choice of alternatives.

(i) the law — one obviously cannot generate illegal alternatives. For example, if your organisation produces poisonous waste and you are making decisions about its disposal, you could not include methods of disposal which contravene the appropriate legislation.

Similarly, shooting intruders may be an appealing alternative in reducing thefts from your factory but would hardly be suitable for inclusion in your list of alternatives.

(ii) Social Responsibility — Most firms are very aware of their social responsibility and for the need to take account of social attitudes. As a result the firm would have to reflect this in their generation of alternative courses of action when dealing with decisions which have social implications. Issues such as pollution, noise, transport of hazardous waste are examples of such issues.

It would be unwise to include alternatives such as:

- emit waste straight into the atmosphere
- do not control noise levels
- transport high toxic waste in the boots of cars.

Social pressure either real or perceived will force the exclusion of these alternatives and the inclusion of others which are felt more suitable.

(iii) Company Practice. It may well be the practice of the company to do or not do certain things. For example, the company may insist on "buying British" and hence an alternative course of action which involved purchasing a German machine guard would not be acceptable.

These limitations on your choice of alternatives are all external in the sense that you have very little control over them. You may generate a very wide list of alternatives only to find that some cannot be included for reasons outwith your control.

Internal Limitations

Internal factors which can limit your choice of alternatives are much more difficult to identify and illustrate.

We have probably all experienced some time when we have worked on a problem for several days or hours and when discussing it with someone else, he or she comes up with some completely new point. "Why did I not think of that? I've been working on this for days and didn't see that point of view!" These reactions are all too common.

The fact that they are common should be some consolation. Most people experience this at some time or other. We can be so close to a problem that we don't see all the relevant factors. Equally worrying is when we are presented with some problem and others always seem to be much more incisive in their thinking than we are. They are probably thinking the same about you!

The fact is that we are all different and do approach problems differently. We must accept this and try to minimise the risk of omitting some important alternative. Remember that if the alternative which will lead to the best decision is left out then the best decision cannot be taken at the end of the day.

Our lack of ability or limited ability to generate all relevant and reasonable alternatives must be acknowledged before we can begin to resolve the problems it will cause.

We could, for example, leave the decision problem for a day or two and come back to it later hoping for fresh insight. Alternatively we could share the problem with a number of others in the hope that the collective wisdom will produce all reasonable alternatives.

What we have to try to do is to think without blinkers on, to grasp the whole of a problem and not let our thinking be constrained in any false way.

One useful illustration of how simple it is to fall into the trap of blinkered thinking is this old problem. (The author can take no credit for this puzzle nor can they give credit as the origins of it are not clear).

47

The task is to draw four straight lines which will pass through all nine dots once. The only conditions are that once you start you are not allowed to lift your pencil off the paper until after the fourth straight line has been drawn or go back over a line already drawn:

```
    •   •   •

    •   •   •

    •   •   •
```

See how you manage! I think you will find the task fairly difficult. So that you don't become neurotic completely we have included the solution at the end of this chapter. You are, of course, on your honour not to sneak a look at this solution even just to "confirm your ideas!"

3.4.3 States of Nature

All that we have said about alternatives applies equally to the generation of states of nature.

● We must identify all possible and reasonable states and accept that there will be limitations:

— external — factors beyond our control which prohibit the inclusion of certain states. For example, some uncertainty which is now certain, possibly because of statute or social pressure.

— internal — psychological barriers to contemplating uncertainties.

Rather than go over the same ground we have just covered for alternatives let us look at some unique factors about states of nature.

(i) How do we go about quantifying uncertainty?

What are the chances of there being a small fire, a large fire, of the control device controlling the fire or not? We have to fall back on probabilities. We covered this topic fairly fully in the course on Risk Analysis and we will say a little more about the application of probability to decision making as we move on to look at decision analysis.

(ii) The number of States of Nature

We have mentioned already that there will be an almost infinite number of states in many problems. If we take the insurance purchasing example then we could have no fire at all or a fire of any magnitude. There are hundreds or thousands of different severities we could have.

It is here we may have to group states of nature into broad bands or indeed use some kind of computer analysis to assist us.

(iii) The Root of Uncertainty

The states of nature are regarded as uncertain states only because we have imperfect knowledge about what is going to happen in the future. If we knew perfectly what was going to take place then there would be no problem of uncertainty. We have already mentioned this earlier but it is an important concept to grasp.

It is our lack of knowledge which is really at the root of the uncertainty and no matter what we do we will never have perfect knowledge. The best we can do is to increase our knowledge by reducing the imperfections. We could, for example, employ fire engineers to advise us on how effective the fire control devices will be, we could consult economists to help in our forecasts about the state of the economy. These steps will not lead to perfect knowledge, they simply add a bit more information to our own.

As we move on to analyse decisions in the next chapter we will see that much of the effort will revolve around the value of information and the benefit we derive from having it.

3.4.4 Pay-offs

The pay-offs represent the final component of the structure of decision. We have a comprehensive list of alternatives and have worked out all the possible states of nature. We then must decide what measurement we are going to put against each alternative and state of nature combination. In other words, what measure or factor will we select to tell us how good or efficient each alternative is when related to each state of nature.

In the simple investment example we used earlier we chose the return on the investment as a pay-off. This gave us nine different pay-offs, corresponding to the nine alternative/state of nature combinations. Once these nine pay-offs were inserted in the matrix we were then in a position to begin to decide which alternative to select.

Let us create a risk management example and try to pick up a few of the points we have mentioned so far. A company is reviewing its insurance cover for one particular form of risk and has decided that it has three courses of action open to it. It may insure in full, insure with a £20,000 aggregate deductible or not insure at all.

Having reviewed the statistics for previous years the company has generated three states of nature. The first is that there will be no losses at all during the year, the second is that there will be a moderate level of losses which in the aggregate will be about £15,000 and the final state is that losses may run at a high level which will produce an aggregate total of £100,000. Clearly there would have to be very many states of nature to take account of all possibilities but three will suffice for the sake of illustration.

When the matrix is drawn it will look like:

	No losses	Medium losses £15,000	High level of losses £100,000
Full insurance			
Insurance with aggregate deductible £20,000			
No insurance			

The question now is what figures to put in the grid to complete the matrix.

In risk management terms we are usually talking about negative values rather than positive in-flows of funds. In many other decisions the decision maker will know his costs and the expected financial benefit and can work out some kind of net result. Some alternatives may be more costly than others and yet yield high returns, some less expensive alternatives may take much longer to produce any reasonable return.

All these factors can usually be measured and the net effect or net contribution to profits can be measured.

In risk management decisions, nine times out of ten, we have the age old problem of working in negatives. We are spending money in the hope of minimising loss. It is invariably impossible to measure what is saved, i.e. fires which did not happen, staff who were not injured, goods which did not cause damage etc., etc.

In most cases we are concerned with minimising loss amounts, we are usually in the business of reducing negatives rather than increasing positives. In the insurance example we could have a pay-off which is the net cost to the company. For example if we insured in full what would this cost? If we had no insurance what would this cost? Provided all entries on the matrix are consistent and as long as we define the pay-offs then we are alright.

In our example if we say that full insurance would be £3,500 and insurance with the deductible would be £3,000 then we would end up with a matrix looking like this:

	No losses	(Aggregate) Medium losses £15,000	(Aggregate) High level of losses £100,000
Full insurance	3,500	3,500	3,500
Insurance with aggregate deductible £20,000	3,000	18,000	23,000
No insurance	0	15,000	100,000

We can see now that the alternative of full insurance will give the same premium regardless of the state of nature. Insuring with the £20,000 aggregate deductible will mean that if losses only sum to £15,000 then we will have to meet them in total and of course pay the premium of £3,000. Should the losses sum to £100,000 then we benefit from the policy and will only pay the £20,000 deductible plus, of course, the £3,000 premium.

Should we decide to buy no insurance then we will have to bear the full cost of any losses.

Not all of our decision problems will involve money as a pay-off and so let us just conclude this chapter by looking at the two basic forms of pay-off measure.

(i) Firstly we can have pay-offs with a natural measure. Money is an example. A natural measure is one which is objective and about which there can be no argument.

Money is the most common but we could also have measures such as, the number of claims, hours lost in accidents, units damaged in production and so on.

The main point to remember is that we define the measure exactly so that there is no ambiguity.

(ii) Secondly we could imagine a number of pay-offs which have no natural or objective measure. For example, attitudes of a workforce toward some new safety apparatus has no natural pay-off. How a local community may react to some new development at your plant cannot be measured objectively.

In these instances we would have to try to find some kind of numerical measure to include in the analysis of the decision. We could possibly issue some kind of questionnaire or speak to staff in order to get some feel for how they felt. We may ask them to rank certain alternatives but whatever we do, we will end up with some contrived measure.

This brings us to the end of our examination of the structure of decisions. We have looked at the place of uncertainty in business decision making and at the individual components of alternative courses of action, states of nature and pay-offs.

Not every decision you face will be the same basic shape as the one we have discussed, or will include the same elements in the same manner as we have examined them. It is hoped however that sufficient information has been given for you to apply appropriate techniques to actual decision problems.

Now that we understand what makes a decision and have all the necessary information to complete the structure, we are left with the task of actually taking the decision. Now we must select one of the alternatives. In chapter four we move on to look at various ways of deciding which alternative to select.

Puzzle Solution

The problem was given in the context of not being able to think without blinkers about problems. Most of you will have found that you would have completed the task easily if you were only allowed to lift your pencil off the paper once, or permitted five lines instead of four.

The solution is:

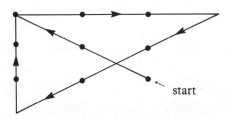

The solution involved going right outside the box created by the nine dots. Most of us will have falsely created a kind of barrier and will not have wanted to go beyond the square.

Chapter 4

DECISION ANALYSIS FOR RISK MANAGEMENT I

4.0   In chapter three we examined, in some detail, all the components in the structure of a decision. We started with the basic idea of problem recognition and progressed through definition of the problem, stating objectives, searching for alternatives and states of nature to measuring pay-offs. In the end we had established a simple decision matrix which we felt represented our problem of decision making under uncertainty.

What we did not do was to suggest how the problem should be resolved. We gave no clue as to how to solve the decision problem. It is to this topic we turn in chapter four. In short, we are now at the stage when we must decide how to decide.

We have a list of possible alternative courses of action, a comprehensive idea of all the states of nature which may play upon the problem, we have defined the pay-off and now we have to take a decision. Which alternative will we select? How will we decide which alternative to select? Clearly, we are in need of some kind of solution strategy. We need a criterion or criteria which we may use to help in the task of selecting an alternative.

Before becoming too involved in examining potential criteria, let us create a basic decision problem which we can use throughout this chapter and expand upon as we introduce new concepts.

The problem we will use as an illustration concerns a departmental store. A company which owns a number of large department stores has become increasingly concerned at the level of shrinkage it is experiencing. Shrinkage is the term used to describe both shoplifting and staff thefts. Shrinkage has now reached a level where some serious action is required on the part of general management.

The risk manager has been making different recommendations for some years but only recently has management realised that the shrinkage rate is moving ahead of what might be regarded as the norm for the retailing sector.

The general manager has instructed the risk manager to implement suitable risk control techniques with a view to reducing the level of shrinkage.

The risk manager is obviously pleased that finally some action is to be taken, however he is undecided as to what control mechanism would be "best". He has narrowed down the control techniques to three; retaining a security firm to provide store detectives, leasing T.V. scanners to cover the shop floor and staff areas and finally marking each garment with a sensitised dot which, if not removed by sales staff, will activate a bell when taken out of the department. There were a number of other alternatives which have all been discounted for one reason or another.

The risk manager has considered that each one of these alternatives will now have definite pay-offs or outcomes. The outcome will depend on how efficient the method is in controlling the shrinkage risk. How efficient the method is, does in turn depend on whether the rate of shrinkage stays the same as it is at the moment, rises to a higher level or falls. (At this stage any author of text book examples falls into a serious trap. Readers are bound to be able to think of all kinds of other alternatives and states of nature and all kinds of reasons why the states of nature chosen for the example are less than adequate. The reason for using the illustration is to have a medium through which we can introduce some concepts unfamiliar to the reader. In short, do not get too hung-up on the problem itself, accept its facts at the moment and we will add to these facts as we move on).

We can now draw a simple decision matrix of the decision so far:

	Shrinkage Falls	Shrinkage Static	Shrinkage Rises
Detectives			
T.V. Scanners			
Sensitised Dots			

This is the familiar three by three decision matrix which we developed in chapter two. The alternatives are shown on the left and across the matrix we have the three states of nature. All that remains now is to decide what the pay-off is to be and then complete the nine alternative/state of nature combinations.

(In using the terms "shrinkage rises" and "shrinkage falls" we have not made any quantitative judgement as to what this means. This is not too important for this example but for those who are happier with figures we could say that a rise is a 50% increase and a fall is a 50% decrease).

There are a number of different measures we could use.

● We could measure the total value of shrinkage, given each of the three alternatives and states of nature.

● Alternatively we could measure the *gross* savings which flow from using each alternative. We would calculate the reduction in losses, without regard to the cost of the control mechanism.

● Thirdly we could measure *net* loss savings. This would be the savings or reduction in shrinkage after having taken into account the cost of the mechanism itself.

There are arguments in favour of each of these measures but we will select the third. The first one, which concentrated on the value of losses would be interesting but in the end we would have a matrix of large figures, which may even be added to by the cost of the control mechanism itself. These large figures would be in the form of negative amounts of money and so we would be endeavouring to *minimise* the pay-off. It somehow seems more appropriate to *maximise* return.

The second measure takes no account of the cost of achieving the savings and so is really not a viable option. The return we get from any alternative is only obtained at some cost and to ignore cost would give an unrealistic picture. We could, for example, have an alternative which involved employing hundreds of store detectives, marking each garment with the sensitised dot and using the T.V. scanners. The costs would be extraordinarily high but the savings may be high too. To ignore the cost is unrealistic.

The third method of measuring pay-off does take into account the cost and also allows us to think in terms of maximising return. This is really no different from most other business decisions. The person making the decision is involved in spending money in the hope of making some contribution to profit. In this example the risk manager hopes to contribute to profit by reducing the level of shrinkage. He has to spend some money to do this but in the end looks for a return.

What we need then are some figures to calculate the pay-off. Let us say that he has negotiated with a security firm, the provision of a certain number of store detectives on a one year contract. The cost of the contract, in total, is £20,000. It is estimated that the use of these detectives will save £30,000 in the year mainly from shoplifting. The effectiveness of the detectives will not vary, it is suggested, with the rate of shrinkage. The £30,000 savings will remain static no matter what happens to the overall rate of shrinkage, this is largely due to the fact that the savings are made from the 'marginal' or 'casual' shoplifter who will be deterred by the knowledge that detectives are at work. While the overall rate of shrinkage may rise or fall, the block of casual shoplifters will remain reasonably constant.

The T.V. scanners can be leased for £15,000 and the savings in losses will vary quite a bit depending upon what happens to the rate of shrinkage. If shrinkage remains at its current level, it is expected that the savings will be £30,000. This is the same as the store detectives. However if shrinkage rises then the savings increase to £42,000. This is due to the efficiency of the cameras in both deterring people and "spotting" people regardless of the level of shrinkage. Should the level of shrinkage decrease then the savings drop to £18,000. The T.V. scanners need a good level of activity to prove their worth and do not seem to be as much of a deterrent as the detectives.

Using the dots is the cheapest method. The garments in the store can be marked at a cost of £10,000 over the next year. It is anticipated that this would save £25,000 on the current rate of shrinkage. If shrinkage rises then the savings increase to a figure of £40,000. However a low level of shrinkage would render the method fairly impotent and the savings are estimated at no more than £7,000.

These are the basic figures we need to decide what the pay-off is for each combination of alternative and state of nature. In the matrix below we have shown the savings we expect in losses and the cost of achieving these savings, with the net figure in brackets.

	Shrinkage falls	Shrinkage static	Shrinkage rises
Detectives	30,000-20,000 (10,000)	30,000-20,000 (10,000)	30,000-20,000 (10,000)
T.V. Scanners	18,000-15,000 (3,000)	30,000-15,000 (15,000)	(42,000-15,000) (27,000)
Sensitised Dots	7,000-10,000 (−3,000)	25,000-10,000 (15,000)	40,000-10,000 (30,000)

We can tidy this up now and present our final matrix with all the pay-offs shown as single figures.

	Shrinkage falls	Shrinkage static	Shrinkage rises
Detectives	10,000	10,000	10,000
T.V. Scanners	3,000	15,000	27,000
Sensitised Dots	−3,000	15,000	30,000

This then is the shape of the basic decision problem. What we have to do now is to decide upon a method of selecting one of the three alternatives. In general terms we could divide the various criteria we could adopt into probabilistic and non-probabilistic.

4.1   Non-Probabilistic Decision Criteria

Looking at the decision matrix we can see the classic dilemma. If shrinkage rises then we should go for the sensitised dots. On the other hand if shrinkage should reduce then the best option would be the detectives. Should the level of shrinkage stay the same as it is at the moment then we would have to decide between the T.V. Scanners and the sensitised dots.

The difficulty is that we do not know what state of nature is going to apply in the future but yet we have to make the decision now. Our lack of information about the future is the seed of our uncertainty. If we only knew what was going to happen we would always take the best decision, however we invariably do not have perfect knowledge of how things will end up in a year's time and hence we can only work to a criterion at this present time.

4.1.1   Criterion of Pessimism (Maximin)

This criterion imagines that the worst state of nature will occur and then urges you to maximise your position assuming that this has happened. In other words we are maximising under the minimum conditions, maximin.

The worst state of nature, not the worst or lowest pay-off, is that shrinkage levels will generally increase. This is the least advantageous state of nature. The pay-offs, under this worst state of nature would then be:

	Shrinkage Rises
Detectives	10,000
T.V. Scanners	27,000
Sensitised Dots	30,000

The best alternative to select, given this worst state of nature is clearly the sensitised dots. If we went for this alternative *and* the level of shrinkage rises then we will have maximised our position.

4.1.2   Criterion of Optimism (Maximax)

The opposite of pessimism is optimism and so our next criterion is one based on the best state of nature. We now assume that the best will occur and we will want to maximise our position in this maximum state, maximax.

The best state of nature would be that the level of shrinkage falls:

	Shrinkage Falls
Detectives	10,000
T.V. Scanners	3,000
Sensitised Dots	−3,000

The best alternative which maximises our return in this case would be the use of detectives.

One slight modification to this basic criterion of optimism is to place some measure on how optimistic you feel. There is no really objective way to arrive at a figure for how optimistic you feel. You may have some previous experience or just have a feeling that shrinkage will fall. Let us say that we are 80% sure shrinkage will fall. What we do is to say that the opposite state of nature, that shrinkage will rise, has a likelihood of 20%. We can use these figures to get some measure of the effect of our feeling of optimism.

We are 80% sure that shrinkage will fall and 20% sure that it will rise. As a result we feel we have an 80% chance of getting savings of £3,000, for example, if we use the T.V. Scanners and a 20% chance of having savings of £27,000 if the level of shrinkage rises. In the long run therefore we could expect savings of £7,800 (£3,000 x 0.8 + £27,000 x 0.2). (We are going to say much more about probabilities and calculations like this, later).

For all three alternatives the calculations would therefore be:

	80% Shrinkage Falls.		20% Shrinkage Rises.
Detectives	10,000 x 0.8	+	10,000 x 0.2 = 10,000
T.V.Scanners	3,000x 0.8	+	27,000 x 0.2 = 7,800
Sensitised Dots	−3,000 x 0.8	+	30,000 x 0.2 = 3,600

In the light of these calculations we would select the detectives as they lead to savings of £10,000, which is the highest.

You can see that the different alternatives would have different chances of being selected by you, depending upon how optimistic you feel. One of the values of this idea of arriving at a coefficient of optimism such as the 80% figure is that you can now test the data to see when you would cease to prefer one alternative in favour of another.

For example you could calculate how optimistic you would have to be that shrinkage will fall, before you would move from preferring detectives to preferring the T.V. Scanners. When we look at the matrix it is obvious that no matter how high or low our coefficient of optimism is, the end result will always be £10,000. This is because £10,000 is the pay-off in the best *and* the worst state.

As a result, any other alternative would have to exceed £10,000 if it was to be preferred to the use of detectives. By letting the coefficient of optimism be A then we would have, for example:

	Shrinkage Falls		Shrinkage Rises
T.V.Scanners	3,000 x A	+	27,000 x (1-A)>10,000

What this says is that we are multiplying the 3,000 by A which is the measure of how confident we are that shrinkage will fall. The (1-A) is the reciprocal of A, in exactly the same way as the 20% was the reciprocal of the 80% in the earlier example. The result of multiplying 3,000 by A and 27,000 by (1-A) is to exceed, or be greater than, 10,000. It is only if the result is greater than 10,000 that we will prefer that option to the 10,000 we know we get from the use of detectives.

We can solve the equation now and find the value of A:

$$3,000 \times A + 27,000 \times (1-A) > 10,000$$
$$3,000A - 27,000A + 27,000 > 10,000$$
$$-24,000A > -17,000$$
$$A < \frac{-17,000}{-24,000}$$
$$A < 0.7083$$

In other words we have to be less than 70.83% or nearly 71% sure that shrinkage levels are going to fall, before we would move from the first to the second alternative.

We can prove this by inserting 0.7083 for the value of A:
$$3,000 \times 0.7083 + 27,000 \times (1-0.7083)$$
$$= 2124.90 + 7875.90$$
$$= 10,000.80$$

We can round the answer to 10,000 and so we can see that we would have to be almost 71% sure of falling shrinkage just to get the same expected result from T.V. Scanners as we get from using detectives.

The value in being able to manipulate these figures may, for example, lie in your being able either to refute someone's view or indeed support your own. It may be that someone on the management side of your organisation is arguing strongly for the detectives as opposed to the use of T.V. Scanners. If you can get him to say how likely he feels a fall in the levels of shrinkage to be, then you may be able to dismiss his argument. If he says that there is only a 50% chance of shrinkage falling, or some other lower figure if he is trying to put the case for the use of detectives, then you have him. As we have seen, the detectives will only be preferred to the scanners if we are more than 71% sure of falling shrinkage.

4.1.3   The criterion of Regret (Minimax)

The third criterion takes a slightly different view and one which has a certain intuitive appeal. It says simply, "if we select one option with the benefit of hindsight how much will we regret having selected it if it turns out not to have been the best one?"

If the level of shrinkage falls then the best thing to have done would be to have used the detectives. Had we in fact selected one of the other options then we would regret this as the savings would not be as high. In fact the measure of just how much we do regret not selecting the best alternative would be the difference between what we could have saved and what we did save.

	Shrinkage Falls.	Regret
Detectives	10,000	10,000 - 10,000 = 0
T.V.Scanners	3,000	10,000 - 3,000 = 7,000
Sensitised Dots	-3,000	10,000 - (-3,000) = 13,000

Note how we have subtracted what we did save from what we would save under the best alternative given that shrinkage did fall. And so if we had selected the T.V. Scanners we would have savings of £3,000. The best savings were £10,000, had we used the detectives, and so the real measure of our regret is the difference, £10,000-£3,000 or £7,000. We can go through this process for each state of nature and if we do, we end up with a regret matrix as follows:

	Shrinkage Falls	Shrinkage Static	Shrinkage Rises
Detectives	0	5,000	20,000
	(10,000 - 10,000)	(15,000 - 10,000)	(30,000 - 10,000)
T.V.Scanners	7,000	0	3,000
	(10,000 - 3,000)	(15,000 - 15,000)	(30,000 - 27,000)
Sensitised Dots	13,000	0	0
	(10,000 - (-3,000))	(15,000 - 15,000)	(30,000 - 30,000)

The figures in brackets beneath the measure of regret shows how it was arrived at. This then is the regret matrix and what we can do now is adopt a pessimistic mode once more and say, "where do we experience the maximum regrets?"

For detectives this is £20,000, for T.V. scanners is £7,000 and for the dots is £13,000.

	Maximum Regret
Detectives	20,000
T.V.Scanners	7,000
Sensitised Dots	13,000

These are the maximum regret amounts we could experience for each alternative. What we should now try to do is to minimise these maximum regret amounts (minimax). The minimum of the maximum regret amounts is arrived at by selecting the T.V. scanners.

Before leaving these non-probabilistic criteria we could make two points:

1) They are very simplistic. They adopt a basic, simple stance namely optimism, pessimism, and use this as the sole criterion. They can only therefore really be used as a guide. They can act as a foundation for our thinking and may help in discounting certain ideas or in refining others. It is unlikely that they could ever be used as the sole decision solution strategy.

ii) All thoughts of likelihood are ignored, other than the brief mention of coefficients of optimism. The very fact that we are dealing with uncertainty should lead us to consider probabilities and to ignore them is a mistake. Assumptions of certainty are unrealistic in most situations.

This then leads on to the next topic which is the consideration of probabilistic criteria.

4.2   Probabilistic Criteria

We had a brief skirmish with probabilities when we used the coefficient of optimism in some calculations earlier. For those students who are still a bit unfamiliar with probabilities or lack confidence in their ability to use them, it would be a good idea if they referred back to the text on Risk Analysis and did some revision work. We are not going to go into a great deal on the theory of probability as we only want to use probabilities in the narrow context of decision analysis. In the main we are going to concentrate on the role of "Expected Monetary Value" calculations.

In the end we want to use Expected Monetary Value (EMV) calculations in three ways but before we do so let us make some introductory comments on probabilities themselves and on the nature of EMV.

4.2.1   Using Probabilities

There are plenty of people who see no role for probabilities in risk management. A favourite comment of these people is that probability calculations are all very well but the one in a million risk of a catastrophe may be tomorrow.

Such people are harbouring a basic misunderstanding of the nature of probabilities and of the role they can play in assisting risk management decision making. A probability calculation is not the risk manager's equivalent of a crystal ball. A probability calculation is not a prediction of what is going to happen. It is only an estimate. It is intended to throw light on a problem and the decision making process.

When we have large volumes of past data it does seem strange not to try to use it to suggest what may happen in the future. We cannot predict what will happen but an analysis of the likelihood with which certain events have occured or may occur in the future could be useful.

Other people in our organisation may also be using estimates of likelihood. Production engineers may be making reliability calculations, marketing people could be estimating consumer preferences and accountants often forecast future economic trends.

4.2.1   Expected Monetary Value

EMV is simply an application of probabilities where there is some monetary outcome either a gain or a loss. In simple terms we could say that EMV gives us an idea of what an uncertain outcome is worth.

If someone offered to play a game with you where you stood to win £2 if you draw a queen from a pack of cards, how much would you pay to play? The chance of getting a queen is 4 out of 52 or approximately 0.0769. You stand to win £2 if you pick one of these queens but there is less than an 8% chance that you will pick a queen.

You stand to win £2 but there is only a 0.0769 probability that you will.

In other words if you were to play the game a very large number of times then you would win on about eight out of every one hundred shots. What is this game worth to you? How much would you pay for a ticket?

On purely mathematical grounds, ignoring any liking or disliking you may have for gambling, we could say that there is approximately a 7.69% chance of winning £2 and a 92.31% chance of getting nothing. Therefore 7.69% of the time you gain £2 and 92.31% of the time you will have nothing. If you stand to get £2, 7.69% of the time we could say that in the long run you get an average of (£2 x 0.0769), 15.38p rounded down to 15p, each time you play.

As the two outcomes, win or lose, are mutually exclusive you will either get the average figure of 15p, or nothing. Such events are termed alternative events, and if we add them together we could say that in the long run we would expect to win (15p + 0) or 15p for each play of the game. This figure of 15p is the EMV, it is the expected value of the game in monetary terms.

We could illustrate this same point with one more example from the world of games and then use this example as a springboard for illustrating risk management applications of EMV.

Imagine that in an amusement arcade there is a large, electronic wheel of fortune. For a stake of 25p you press a button and the wheel revolves. You win if the wheel stops with the pointer in a winning segment of the wheel. The wheel is shown in Fig. 4.1. (overleaf). There are 100 sections in total and different prizes to be won. Let us work through some arithmetic to answer basic probability questions. The winning segments are gold £5, silver £2, bronze £1 and red 50p.

— What is the chance of winning?

There are 100 sections and of these there are,

1	Gold
3	Silver
5	Bronze
10	Red
81	White

Fig 4.1

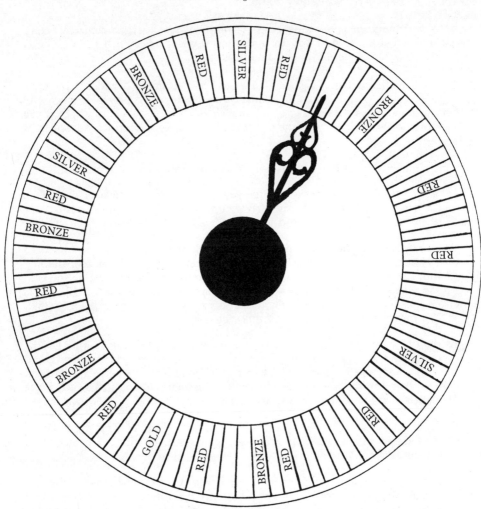

You win if the wheel stops at the non-white sections, and so the various probabilities are,

Gold	1 in 100 or 0.01
Silver	3 in 100 or 0.03
Bronze	5 in 100 or 0.05
Red	10 in 100 or 0.10

The consequence of this is that there is a 19% chance of winning something and add 81% chance of winning nothing.

— How much will you win?

You can win one of four different amounts, either £5, £2, £1, or 50p.

You have a:

          1 in 100 chance of winning £5
          3 in 100 chance of winning £2
          5 in 100 chance of winning £1
       10 in 100 chance of winning 50p

— What can you 'expect' to win?

This is a classic EMV situation. We end up with a list of outcomes and their associated probabilities. All the outcomes are mutually exclusive and so we can find the expected result by combining each outcome with its respective probability and adding them together:

Outcome		Probability	
£5	x	0.01	= 5p
£2	x	0.03	= 6p
£1	x	0.05	= 5p
50p	x	0.10	= 5p
0p	x	0.81	= 0p
			= 21p

The expected monetary value is 21p, and so what does this mean?

i) It is the long run average return per game if you were to play on a very large number of occasions.

ii) The person playing the game would lose in the long run as he or she only recovers 21p for every 25p invested in the game.

iii) The owner of the machine will have to pay out 21p for every 25p received, on average, and so ends up with a return of 4p for each game played.

The long run aspect is worth emphasising, we are not saying you will win 21p tomorrow, the next day or ever. It is the average expected win in the long run.

This simple example did contain some features which we could transfer to the risk management world and to decision making in particular. The key elements in the game were,
- How could I win?
- What are the chances of winning?
- How much will you win?
- What do you expect to win?

We could ask similar questions in a risk management context.

- How could I suffer loss?
- What are the chances of a loss?
- How much could I lose?
- What do I expect to lose?

For example, we could have the following distribution for the cost of accidental damage repairs on our motor fleet.

£'s Cost		p(x)
0<	500	.64
500<	1000	.20
1000<	1500	.15
1500<	2000	.01
		1.00

In the first column we have the cost of claims, let us say up to £2000 which is the level of self retention. In the second column we have the likelihood of losses being in one of the four bands, this is shown as p(x) where 'x' is the financial loss.

This now begins to look very similar to the wheel of fortune problem.

- we will lose if there are accidents
- we can lose any one of a number of different amounts
- we have the chances of losing these amounts
- we can calculate the 'expected' loss.

By taking the mid-point of each range we can now calculate the EMV of losses:

£ Mid-point	p(x)	p(x) mid-point
250	0.64	160
750	0.20	150
1250	0.15	187.50
1750	0.10	17.60
		515

The EMV of each loss is £515. This is the long run expectation over a large number of incidents. It is like an arithmetic mean of the future! We may never actually have a loss of exactly £515 but we would expect losses to average out at this figure over time. We can now use this figure to evaluate insurance premiums, judge suitable deductible levels, decide on the size of any self-funding, measure the worth of any loss prevention steps.

The figure of £515 is not a prediction, it is only an aid to our decision process.

4.3 Applying Probabilities

Let us move on now to look at three ways in which we could use this knowledge of EMV to aid our decision making in general.

4.3.1 EMV as a Decision Criterion

We could incorporate some of the thinking on EMV in the decision matrix framework. The matrix for our shrinkage problem is:

	Shrinkage Falls	Shrinkage Static	Shrinkage Rises
Detectives	10,000	10,000	10,000
T.V.Scanners	3,000	15,000	27,000
Sensitised Dots	-3,000	15,000	30,000

Let us say that we have consulted as widely as possible and conclude that there is a 70% chance that shrinkage levels will remain static over the next year. The chance of it rising has been estimated at 0.1 and of falling at 0.2. The probabilities are therefore:

Shrinkage Falls	0.2
Shrinkage Static	0.7
Shrinkage Rises	0.1

This sums to one as the outcomes are mutually exclusive and are also exhaustive of all possibilities. What we can now do is to calculate the EMV of each alternative. This is similar to what we did earlier for the games of chance. For each alternative we know that there are three possible outcomes. Each one of these outcomes has a respective probability of occurring and so we should be able to calculate the expected outcome.

We do this by multiplying each monetary outcome by the chance that it will occur, then we add the results to get the 'expected' monetary value of that alternative. The calculations are shown below.

	Shrinkage Falls		Shrinkage Static		Shrinkage Rises		EMV of each alternative
Detectives	(10000)(0.2)	+	(10000)(0.7)	+	(10000)(0.1)		= 10000
T.V.Scanners	(3,000)(0.2)	+	(15000)(0.7)	+	(27000)(0.1)		= 13800
Sensitised Dots	(-3000)(0.2)	+	(15000)(0.7)	+	(30000)(0.1)		= 12900

This calculation shows that the highest 'expected' savings, £13800, arise from using the T.V.Scanners. This is not to say that using the scanners *will* produce the highest actual savings, but based on the figures we have at the moment this is what we would expect in the long term.

It is a decision criterion, no more than that, but it is our aid to deciding. In the absence of an aid such as this we would have to reply on much more subjective criteria. We can now take this information and combine it with any other information we have, based on our experience, and take the final decision.

4.3.2   Finding Optimum Probabilities

The second use to which we can put our knowledge of EMV is in finding optimum probabilities given two mutually exclusive states of nature. Let us say that we have reduced the states of nature in our problem to two:
- Shrinkage will be static or fall
- Shrinkage will rise.

We have re-calculated the pay-offs for these two states of nature in respect of the three alternatives and now have:

	Shrinkage static or falls	Shrinkage rises
a1 Detectives	10000	10000
a2 T.V.Scanners	9000	21000
a3 Sensitised Dots	6000	23000

(How the new pay-offs were obtained is not too important but in this case we simply took an average e.g., to get the T.V. Scanners outcomes we averaged the outcomes for a falling and static shrinkage (i.e., 3,000 + 15,000 dividend by 2) to get 9,000 and then averaged the static and rises figure (i.e., 15000 + 27000 dividend by 2) to get 21000).

With these figures, we can now plot a graph as shown in Fig. 4.2.

Fig 4.2

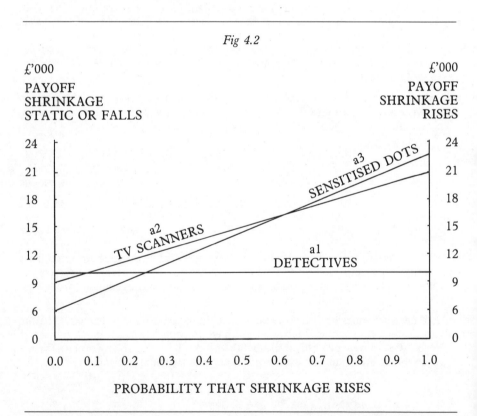

PROBABILITY THAT SHRINKAGE RISES

On the two vertical axes we have measured the pay-offs which will follow under the two States of Nature. The horizontal axis measures probability, in this case the probability of shrinkage rising. The whole difficulty is that we do not know what the probability of either state occurring is. What we do know is that if shrinkage rises then the outcomes will be 10000, 21000 and 23000 for the three outcomes of detectives, T.V. Scanners and Sensitised Dots. If shrinkage definitely rises then the probability of rising shrinkage would be 1, and so we have plotted the pay-off for each alternative on the right hand vertical axis which corresponds to certainty.

If shrinkage does *not* rise then it will have fallen or remained static and so we have plotted the outcome for the three alternatives, in this state of nature on the left hand vertical axis corresponding to a probability of O. We then joined these plotted points by three straight lines.

We can look at some interpretations of this picture now.

a) we can see that the sensitised dots alternative will always be preferred provided that the probability of shrinkage rising is greater than 0.6. We can see this because the line for this alternative is higher than the other lines for that section of the graph where the probability is greater than 0.6. The line indicates the pay-off and so when the a3 line crosses above the a2 line then the pay-off is higher.

We can test the accuracy of this alternative by calculating the EMV of the two alternatives, a2 and a3 if the probability of shrinkage rising is 0.6.

	Shrinkage static or falls		Shrinkage rises
T.V. Scanners	(9000)(0.4)	+	(21000)(0.6) = 16200
Sensitised Dots	(6000)(0.4)	+	(23000)(0.6) = 16200

The two EMV's are the same as the probability of rising shrinkage is 0.6. We would find it hard to distinguish between the two alternatives, purely on the basis of their EMV.

Notice that if the probability of rising shrinkage was 0.7 then the result would be:

	Shrinkage static or falls		Shrinkage rises
T.V.Scanners	(9000)(0.3)	+	(21000)(0.7) = 17400
Sensitised Dots	(6000)(0.3)	+	(23000)(0.7) = 17900

And so if the probability rises from 0.6 to 0.7 we begin to see a change in the EMV's.

This could be useful in defending one or other of the risk control schemes. On objective grounds you would have to be more than 60% sure that shrinkage was rising before you could justify the expense of marking each garment with the sensitised dots.

b) we can see secondly, that the T.V. Scanners will be preferred to the other alternatives provided the probability of rising shrinkage is between about 0.07 and 0.6. Over this range of probabilities the a2 line is higher than the other two, thus yielding the highest pay-off.

c) the third finding we could establish from the graph is that a3 is the least preferred alternative if you believe that the probability of shrinkage rising is less than 0.25. In other words if you are at least 75% sure that shrinkage will stay the same or fall then the sensitised dots is not the optimum alternative.

d) Fourthly we can see that the detectives will only yield the highest EMV when you are almost sure that the rate of shrinkage is static or falling.

These interpretations may be useful in discussion with others about the merit of the various risk reduction mechanisms. It is particularly valuable if you have already had some indication from others of their feeling about the likely shift in the level of shrinkage. Their views can then either be used against them, when looking at the graph, or used to support their view. For example if one store manager has already indicated that in his view shrinkage is on the way down, then this would be incompatible with the desire to mark garments with dots.

4.3.3   Evaluation of Information

We have said earlier that one of the major problems in the whole area of decision making under uncertainty is that we have imperfect information about what is going to happen in the future. This imperfection in our knowledge is what produces the uncertainty and is what could cause us to take a wrong, or less than optimum, decision.

What we can do to help our lack of knowledge is to buy assistance to reduce the imperfection. We can see practical examples of this in the seismic testing carried out by oil exploration companies, the market research carried out on behalf of the producers of consumer goods, the pilot testing of television programmes and so on. These steps are intended to provide a little more information and so reduce the area of uncertainty.

Our knowledge of EMV can be used to assist us in deciding just how much such information is worth.

Let us create another simple example with which to illustrate the point. Someone will play a game with you. He will toss a coin and if it lands heads up you win £20 and if it lands tails up you will win nothing. It will cost you £2.50 to play. Don't decide whether you will play or not. Instead, imagine that there is a third person who has a crystal ball which is 100% accurate in all the predictions it makes. He is entirely independent of you and the person asking you to play the game and sells information about the future. How much would you pay this third person for information about the future. How much would you pay him for information about the outcome of the next flip of the coin? Remember, he is always correct in his predictions and so if you pay him you *will* find out what is about to happen and so will have *perfect* knowledge about the future. What is the most you would be prepared to pay for this information? Write the amount down somewhere on a piece of paper.

Let us use our knowledge of EMV to try and establish what we may expect from the various options open to us.

Firstly, what is the position if we do *not* use the fortune teller? We have a straightforward decision as to whether to play or not. We can write it in the form of the matrix with which are now familiar.

68

	Win		Lose
Play	20(0.5)	+	0(0.5) = £10
Don't play	0(0.5)	+	0(0.5) = £0

The EMV of not playing is of course O and of playing is £10. We will of course only gain £10 if we had paid to play the game and so we should really deduct the stake of £2.50 which leaves us with an expected return of £7.50.

(Just as an aside, some may wonder why we didn't deduct the stake from the £20 before multiplying it by the 0.5. Can you see why this would be wrong? The stake is paid regardless of winning or losing and so is not really part of the EMV calculation. If you wanted to do it this way, you would have to deduct £2.50 from the £20 and deduct £2.50 from the £0. This seems a bit artificial!).

The highest 'expected' return is £7.50 and on this basis we would be willing to play.

Now, what about the option of seeking perfect information. In this case we are not faced with a decision, as we have decided to seek out information. What we are faced with is the same uncertainty about the outcome. This is an important point to grasp. Say that you consult the fortune teller and he says the coin will land heads up. In this case you will definitely play and consequently win £20. However, you may have consulted him and he said the coin was going to land tails up. In such a case you would not play and consequently would win nothing. In other words you would play when he said you would win and not play when he said you would lose. This makes sense, it is the reason you consulted him in the first place.

The point to note is that the fortune teller does not **control** the outcome, he only **predicts** it. In view of this, what do you expect to be the outcome if you consult him. In the long run he will predict heads, half the time and tails half the time. And so you would play half the time and not play half the time. We have another expected monetary value calculation:

	Play		Don't play
Consult fortune teller	(20-2.50)(0.5)	+	(0)(0.5) = 8.75

the expected value is now £8.75 with the advantage of perfect information.

(This time we have deducted the stake from the potential winnings as you will only pay the stake on half of all occasions. This is unlike the first example where you pay the stake irrespective of winning or losing. In this example you only pay the stake when you know you are getting the £20. The net gain is therefore £17.50, which will you get half of the time).

We now have the EMV with no information and the EMV with perfect information. The 'expected' value of this perfect information is therefore the difference between these two figures.

Expected value of perfect information	=	Expected value with perfect information	-	Expected value with no information.

$$EVP1 = £8.75 - £7.50$$
$$EVP1 = £1.25$$

The maximum advantage you gain from having this perfect insight into the future is £1.25 per play. Look back now to see what you answered to the original question as to how much you would be prepared to pay. Was it more or less than £1.25?

Even with perfect knowledge we would not pay more than £1.25 and so if someone came to us saying they make pretty good guesses about the outcomes of coin flips we would pay them no more than £1.25.

You can see that this calculation, although very theoretical in nature, does give us some ceiling on the maximum we should be prepared to spend on reducing the imperfection in our knowledge.

We can go on now to apply these ideas to our example of the shrinkage problem. We had the original matrix which looked like this.

	Shrinkage Falls (0.2)	Shrinkage Static (0.7)	Shrinkage Rises (0.1)
Detectives	10,000	10,000	10,000
T.V.Scanners	3,000	15,000	27,000
Sensitised Dots	-3,000	15,000	30,000

When we used the EMV to find the optimum alternative you will recall that the three EMV's were:

Detectives	10,000
TV Scanners	13,800
Sensitised Dots	12,900

The optimum decision was to select the T.V. Scanners as this gave us the highest 'expected' return of the three alternatives. This is similar to the straight forward tossing of a coin example we used above. In that example the highest EMV was associated with playing the game where you could win £20 or nothing on the toss of a coin.

What we want to know now is how much we would pay for perfect information about the future. In our example this would be perfect information about what was going to happen to the level of shrinkage. We can find the maximum we should be prepared to pay by assuming that perfect information about the future is available.

If such perfect information was available then we would always know which state of nature was going to occur and would always select the alternative which gave us the highest return, under that state of nature. For example, if we know that the level of shrinkage was going to fall then we would select the detectives as this gives a saving of £10,000. If we had certain knowledge that the rate of shrinkage was to remain static then we would select either the T.V. Scanners or the sensitised dots. Given perfect information that the level of shrinkage was rising then we would select the sensitised dots.

The point to remember at this stage, the same point we mentioned earlier, is that the possession of *perfect* information only tells you what will happen, it does not *determine* what *will* happen. And so if we had perfect knowledge about the rate of shrinkage we would know if it was going to rise, fall or stay the same. We cannot *make* it rise, fall or stay the same.

The person with this perfect knowledge is always correct and so 20% of the time he will say the level of shrinkage is going down, 70% of the time he will say it is going to remain static and 10% of the time he will say that it will rise. As we will always select the optimum alternative for the state of nature which we say will apply, we will;
either, Select detectives 20%, of the time for savings of £10,000
or, Select either the TV or Dots 70% of the time for savings of £15,000
or, Select dots 10% of the time for savings of £30,000

In other words the expected value with perfect information is:

$$(10,000)(0.2) + (15,000)(0.7) + (30,000)(0.1) = £15,500$$

With the advantage of perfect information about the future we now have an 'expected' monetary value of £15,500. By comparing this to the EMV with no knowledge, we can get a measure of the value of perfect information.

Expected value of perfect information	=	Expected value with perfect information	-	Expected value with no information.

$$\begin{aligned} \text{EVP1} &= £15,500 = £13,800 \\ \text{EVP1} &= £1,700 \end{aligned}$$

And so, even if perfect information was available to us as to which state of nature would apply, we would not spend more than £1,700 to obtain it.

Unfortunately perfect information does not exist in the real world and we must rely on buying imperfect knowledge as we have said earlier. We may employ a security consultant to advise on how best we should proceed but in the end his knowledge is not perfect. We will have to find a way to value this imperfect knowledge and will do so after we have introduced one more concept.

Chapter 5

DECISION ANALYSIS FOR RISK MANAGEMENT II

5.0   We concluded the previous chapter by saying that perfect information is really a theoretical concept. In the real world all we can hope for is that there is some way in which we can reduce the uncertainty we have about the future. One way we can do this is to purchase information which, while it is not 'perfect', is nevertheless valuable to us.

We are going to move on to look at a technique which can be used to value the benefit that such information may yield. The particular technique is known as Bayesian analysis. Before we can do this we have to consider one additional concept.

5.1   Decision Trees

A decision tree has a value in its own right, quite apart from the use to which we will put it in the context of measuring the value of information. This section will look at the use of such trees and then in section 5.2 we will return to the issue of valuing information, the discipline required in building decision trees is a useful discipline to acquire.

A simple tree for our decision on shrinkage is shown in Fig. 5.1

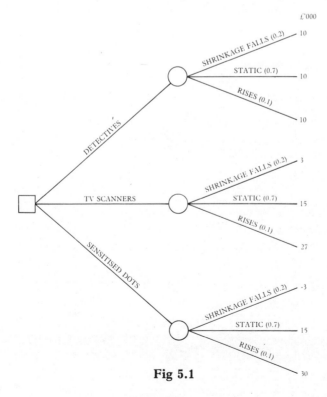

Fig 5.1

73

This is exactly the same decision as was illustrated in the matrix. This time we have drawn a tree and followed certain conventions in doing so.

- The tree moves from left to right. It could just as easily move from bottom to top, top to bottom or right to left, but it does seem easier, to many, to read from left to right.

- Decisions are indicated by a square. These are referred to as decision nodes.

- Chance events are depicted by a circle. These chance nodes correspond to the various states of nature.

- The outcome of each alternative and state of nature combination is shown at the tip of the branches of the tree.

- The probabilities with which chance events occur are shown in brackets on the relevant branch of the tree.

To carry out any analysis on the tree we have to perform an operation known as 'averaging out and rolling back'. We can see the effect of this in Fig. 5.2.

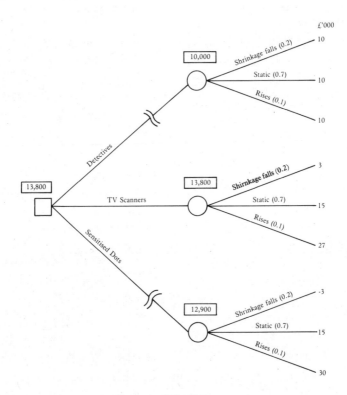

Fig 5.2

We can see that at the very beginning of the tree we are faced with the decision as to which of the three alternatives to select. Regardless of which road we go down we are then faced with the chance that levels of shrinkage may rise, fall or remain static. In averaging out we have calculated the EMV for each of the three main alternatives and displayed these in boxes above the relevant chance node. What these do is to act as signs at the end of each initial branch of the tree. If you are standing at the lefthand side of the tree, ready to take a decision, and you look down each of the pathways open to you then you will see the three different signs. Obviously, you will select the path which indicates the highest expected return and go down it.

Calculating the three EMV's is the averaging out process and blocking off the two less attractive alternatives is the rolling back.

We can now extend this simple problem and see how the tree can cope with it. Let us say that the risk manager has been looking at the whole problem of shrinkage from a broader perspective and in consultation with the store manager has had some new thoughts. They think that a modification of the store layout could reduce the overall level of shrinkage, and make the reduction techniques even more effective. In fact they decide that the gross savings could be increased by 50% in each case. (We will interpret this as meaning that the -£3,000 outcome, if we used the sensitised dots *and* the level of shrinkage falls, will now be -£1,500). The chance of the re-design being successful in reducing shrinkage is estimated at 80%, there is a 50% 'benefit' or 'advantage' to the company in modifying the store layout.

Should the re-design not be successful than the original outcomes will prevail. In either case, success or failure of the re-design to influence levels of shrinkage, the risk manager will still want to consider one of the three risk reduction alternatives. The re-design is going to cost £5,000.

Not re-designing the store layout will leave the risk manager with the same decision he started with at the outset, and is displayed in the tree in Fig. 5.1.

The new tree for the revised decision is shown in Fig. 5.3. (overleaf).

From this figure we can see that our original simple decision has now changed into a more complicated one. The first decision was a single stage problem, an alternative had to be selected and that alternative led to a range of outcomes. In Fig. 5.3 we can see that we are now faced with a multiple stage decision problem. The initial decision is whether or not to re-design the store layout. Once this decision has been taken and an alternative selected we are then confronted with another decision, which alternative risk reduction mechanism to use. You can imagine that certain decisions may have many stages. They can however be displayed in the form of a tree, with each stage of the decision shown clearly and logically.

We can also see from this extended tree that the cost of an alternative can be displayed. On the branch of the tree representing the alternative of re-designing the store we have shown a 'Bridge' over the line which corresponds to the cost of £5,000.

We have averaged out and rolled back the tree, blocking off those alternatives which were not attractive. The expected monetary value is 14.32 or £14,320, if we

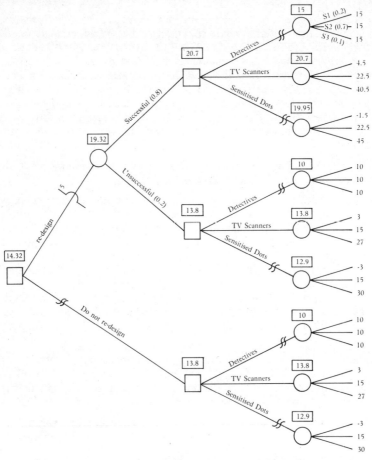

Fig 5.3

select the re-design and then also install the TV scanners. The EMV's are shown in boxes above each chance or decision node.

Looking on the tree as a kind of pathway as we did earlier, we can take the position of someone standing at the very lefthand side of the tree. Looking down the two pathways we can see an expected £19,320 or £13,800. The £19,320 can only be achieved by spending £5,000 and so we are really comparing net expected returns of £14,320 and £13,800. On the basis of this comparison alone, we would prefer to move down the road giving the higher return. Having done so we can then reach a chance node where there is a 20% chance of securing an expected £13,800 and an 80% chance of securing £20,700. Regardless of which chance event occurs we are then faced with a further decision, and so the process continues.

What the tree has done for us is to enable us to project ourselves forward and then reflect this in our decision at this present time. The averaging out of the uncertain amounts and the rolling or folding back to the present time, does produce one preferred alternative.

5.1.1 The value of Information

We have already seen that it is possible to use our knowledge of EMV's to decide the maximum we should spend to add to our knowledge about the future. We said at that time, that perfect knowledge about the future is a theoretical idea. The best we can do is to consult people who know about the matter under consideration and ask for their advice. We could then use their advice to assist our decision making.

5.2 Bayesian Analysis

We will conclude this chapter by looking at a technique which will allow us to do just that. The technique is known as Bayesian Analysis and it will allow us to reflect the findings of new information, in our initial judgement.

The idea behind Bayesian Analysis is intuitively appealing, even if some of the calculations prove less appealing!

- we have some initial assessment of the likelihood of an event occurring.

- we gather some information from other sources.

- we revise our initial assessment in the light of this new information.

We could imagine practical situations where this may apply e.g.,

- you may be deciding to launch a new product and have assessed the chance of it selling well.
  You then employ the services of a market research organisation to carry out some market tests for you. You then revise your initial assessment.

- A company may be considering a decision as to whether or not to drill for oil in a specific location. They have considered the matter carefully and have arrived at an initial assessment of the likelihood that oil exists. They retain a firm of consulting geologists to do extensive testing.
  The oil company then revises its initial assessment.

- A company is planning to export to a new foreign market but require a licence from the foreign government. The company has assessed the likelihood of being granted such a licence on the strength of the evidence it has before it. A firm of political risk analysts are retained to provide additional insight in to the problem.
  The firm then revises its initial judgement.

In each of these examples we have:

i) an initial or prior probability
ii) the gathering of new information
iii) a revised or posterior probability

What is hoped is that a better decision is taken at the end of the day, in the light of the additional information. The difficulty is that the decision to gather extra or new information has to be taken *now* i.e., before it is known whether or not such information is valuable. What we need therefore is a means of measuring the value of this additional information. Bayesian analysis provides us with one way of measuring the value of information.

Before moving on to look at the actual analysis, let us think of one or two risk management situations which could involve the three stages we have observed in the general examples used earlier.

- We could be considering a re-design of our factory layout with a view to reducing the fire risk. We have studied the plans carefully and have assessed the likelihood of fire, given the new layout.

  We then recruit a firm of special fire engineers.
  Subsequently we revise our initial settlement.
- A new piece of machinery has been purchased which has a collapse risk associated with it. We have inspected the machine and made an initial assessment of the likelihood of collapse.
  We ask a firm of consulting engineers to give their view.
  In the light of the new information we revise our initial assessment.
- A new piece of safety apparatus has been suggested to you and you have made an initial assessment as to whether or not it will be accepted by your workforce.
  A pilot test of the apparatus is carried out.
  Your initial assessment is revised in the light of the new information.

In each of the examples we had the same three stages we observed earlier,

i) An initial prior probability
ii) New information
iii) A revised, posterior probability

5.3   Bayesian Formula

What we are looking for is some formula which will enable us to place a value on the information we *can* obtain. If we do this then we can decide whether or not to employ the specialist engineers, carry our pilot tests, retain the services of consultants. We want to know, today, whether or not it is worth acquiring the additional information.

Let us start with a simple example, move on to one which is more practical and then finally return to the main decision on protection against shrinkage.

We will begin with a simple game of chance with which to illustrate some basic points about obtaining 'imperfect' information. We say 'imperfect' as we can never buy 'perfect' information about what is going to happen in the future. Let us say that you can take part in a coin tossing game where, if the coin lands heads up you win £10 but if it lands tails up you lose £4. There is a price to pay and we will think about this in a moment. With this information we can construct a decision tree as in Fig. 5.4. (opposite).

We see the decision as to whether or not we play and then the two chance events, should we decide to play. The EMV is £3 and if we had perfect information we would carry out certain calculations which would allow us to place a ceiling on how much we would be prepared to pay for such information.

In this case we have no crystal ball but there is a person, let us assume, who has a remarkable ability to predict the outcome of coin flips. In fact he has been correct in his predictions on eight out of ten of the predictions made. This has been the case consistently over many years. We can say, therefore, that he has an 80% reliability rate.

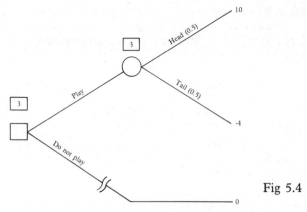

Fig 5.4

What value would this information be to us? How much should we pay for it? We could start working this out by drawing a new decision tree. The first decision now, is whether or not to consult this person. The new tree is in Fig. 5.5.

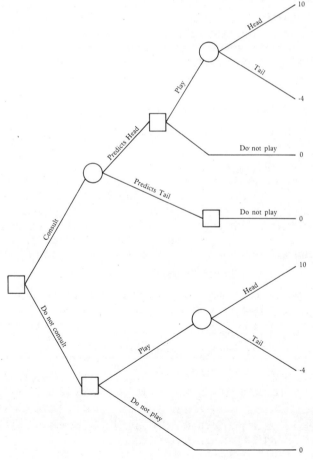

Fig 5.5

We can see from this that we start with the decision of whether or not to consult. If we do not consult then we are left with the same decision as we displayed in the first tree in Fig. 5.4. If we consult, the next stage would be a chance event. We have consulted the person who makes the predictions and he could either predict that the flip of the coin will end in a head or a tail. This chance event is shown in the tree. Should the person predict a tail then we would not play in view of the loss to us, £4. However, if the prediction is a head then we would have to decide whether or not to play, and if we played we could either win or lose. All this is shown in the tree. What is missing are the various probabilities.

There are a number of uncertain events for which probabilities are required. If we decide not to consult the expert then all we need to insert in Fig. 5.4 are the probabilities of a head and tail;

- Probability of a head = P(H) = 0.5
- Probability of a tail = P(T)= 0.5

Should we decide to consult then the first uncertainty is whether the expert will say that the toss of the coin will result in a head or a tail:

- Probability he says a head = P(SH) = ?
- Probability he says a tail = P(ST) = ?

If the expert says that the flip will end in a tail then we will not play. We would however, play if he predicts a head. His prediction does not guarantee a head and so we are faced with the uncertainty that we could get a head or tail, following his prediction of a head:

- The probability of a head given that a head was predicted = P(H/SH) = ?
- The probability of a tail given that a head was predicted = P(T/SH) = ?

We therefore have four probabilities to calculate:

$$P(SH)$$
$$P(ST)$$
$$P(H/SH)$$
$$P(T/SH)$$

Before we can perform any kind of averaging out at the tips of the tree in Fig. 5.5 we will have to establish what the probability of a head and tail are, given that the expert says the flip will end in a head. In other words we need to find:

$$P(H/SH) \text{ and } P(T/SH)$$

The best position we could be in would be that the coin landed heads up and the expert said that the flip would end in a head. In other words:

$$P(H \text{ and } SH)$$

We know from our basic knowledge of probabilities that:

$$P(H \text{ and } SH) = P(H) \, P(SH/H)$$

The event P(H and SH) is, of course, exactly the same as P(SH and H) and so we have,

$$P(H \text{ and } SH) = P(SH \text{ and } H)$$
or $$\quad P(H)P(SH/H) = P(SH)P(H/SH)$$

Remember, what we want to find is the probability that the coin flip will result in a head, given that the experts say it will be a head, P(H/SH).

We can see this in the equation above. We have repeated the equation and underlined P(H/SH),

$$P(H)P(SH/H) = P(SH)\underline{P(H/SH)}$$

In order to find the value of P(H/SH) we will need to restate the equation:

$$P(H/SH) = \frac{P(H)P(SH/H)}{P(SH)}$$

This new formula is simply the earlier one re-ordered to show how P(H/SH) is to be calculated. When we look at this new formula we see the denominator is P(SH). This is the probability that the expert says the flip will result in a head. This can only come about in two ways, *either* the flip results in a head and the expert said it would be a head.

$$P(H \text{ and } SH)$$

or the flip ends in a tail and the expert said it would be a head:

$$P(T \text{ and } SH)$$

Again using our knowledge of probabilities we know that,

$$P(H \text{ and } SH) = P(H)P(SH/H)$$
$$\text{and} \qquad P(T \text{ and } SH) = P(T)P(SH/T)$$

and so we can conclude therefore that P(SH) will come about either by (H and SH) *or* by (T and SH)

$$P(SH) = P(H \text{ and } SH) + P(T \text{ and } SH)$$
$$\text{or} \qquad P(SH) = P(H)P(SH/H) + P(T)P(SH/T)$$

We can now substitute this in the earlier formula;

$$P(H/SH) = \frac{P(H)P(SH/H)}{P(SH)}$$

to get $\quad P(H/SH) = \dfrac{P(H)P(SH/H)}{P(H)P(SH/H) + P(T)P(SH/T)}$

This formula is referred to as Bayes formula and it gives us the probability of an event occurring, given some additional information. We can now calculate the actual probability and average out the trees shown in Fig. 5.5

$$P(H/SH) = \frac{P(H)P(SH/H)}{P(H)P(SH/H) + P(T)P(SH/T)}$$

This is the formula which has to be solved, and from it we can identify the figures we need:

$P(H)$ = the initial probability of a head (0.5)
$P(SH/H)$ = the probability of the expert saying it is a head given that a head is the result of the flip. This is really a measure of how often the expert is correct i.e., predicts a head and it turns out to be a head. We know from what we said earlier that the expert is correct 80%

of the time and so the probability is (0.8).

P(T) = the initial probability of a tail (0.5)

P(SH/T) = this is the chance that the expert predicts a head and the result is a tail. In other words this is the chance that he is wrong (0.2).

When we put these figures in the formula we get:

$$P(H/SH) = \frac{(0.5)(0.8)}{(0.5)(0.8) + (0.5)(0.2)}$$

$$= \frac{0.40}{0.50}$$

$$= 0.8$$

Our initial assessment of the chance of getting a head was 0.5 and we now have an increased figure of 0.8, based solely on the new information we have from the expert. We can now go back and re-draw the tree in Fig.5.5 and insert the new probabilities.

Before doing so we will need to find P(T/SH), P(SH) and P(ST).

P(T/SH) is the chance of getting a tail when the expert said a head would result. This must be 0.2, the reciprocal of 0.8. We can calculate it by the same method as for P(H/SH) just to prove that it is so:

$$P(T/SH) = \frac{P(T)P(SH/T)}{P(T)P(SH/T) + P(H)P(SH/H)}$$

$$= \frac{(0.5)(0.2)}{(0.5)(0.2) + (0.5)(0.8)}$$

$$= \frac{0.10}{0.50}$$

$$= 0.20$$

P(SH) is the probability that the expert predicts a head. We saw earlier:

$$P(SH) = P(H)P(SH/H) = P(T)P(SH/T)$$

and this is exactly what we used in the denominator of the Bayes formula. In other words P(SH) = 0.5. If this is so then P(ST) is 0.5, the reciprocal of P(SH). We can now complete the tree in Fig. 5.5 and insert all the new probabilities.

All the probabilities have been inserted and the effect is that the expected value of the decision is now £3.60 compared to the £3 shown in Fig. 5.4. The expert has been of some value to us but if his services were to cost more than 60p then we would not be prepared to pay for them.

5.4   Practical illustration

The coin tossing example has limited value for us and so we must try to transfer some of the basic ideas to a more realistic illustration.

Let us say that we are considering a scheme to offer private house insurance to the employees of the company for which we are the risk manager. Previously the risk management department only handled the firm's own business and so to begin to offer this insurance service to staff is a major step. (In order to simplify the

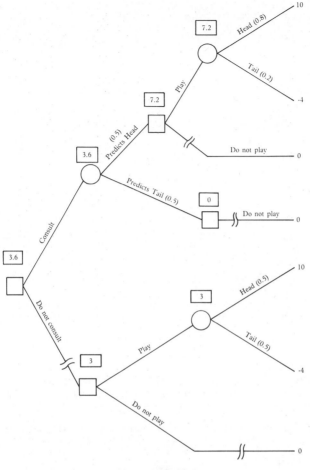

Fig 5.6

illustration we have omitted many of the actual variables which would be included in a real decision of this nature. A decision tree is shown in Fig. 5.7 (overleaf) which represents, in simple terms, the decision before us.

At the moment your department acts as broker for household business on behalf of staff and this provides an income of £60. (This could be £60,000, £6,000 or £600). Should you stop doing this and decide to offer the new scheme then you could gain £100 if the take up rate among staff is very high or only gain £50 if the take up rate is low. Offering the scheme implies that you would no longer act as a broker and so it is a decision between the certain £60 on the one hand and the possibility of either £100 or £50 if you start the scheme.

We can see from the simple tree that the averaging out process results in an expected monetary value of £95. We can either offer the scheme to staff or not. If we don't then we have the return of £60 which comes from current commission

83

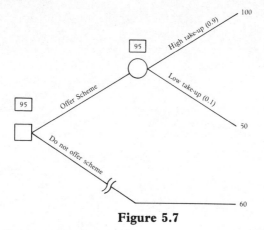

Figure 5.7

income. By offering the scheme we have an expected return of £95 which is shown above the chance node. We, therefore, decide to block off the "don't offer the scheme" path and go for offering it to staff. The expected £95 is the result of averaging the two outcomes, the £100 if there is a high take up and the £50 if the take up is low. These two outcomes arise with a probability of 0.9 and 0.1 respectively. These are our own initial probabilities and what we want to do now is to gather some additional, more expert advice, which may lead us to revise them.

This is the classic Bayesian situation, we have a prior probability and now want to calculate a posterior probability based on some additional information. Let us say that a market research consultancy can carry out a study among a sample of staff to gauge their reaction to the new scheme. The intention of recruiting the consultancy is to see whether or not there is evidence that the staff would favour the scheme and hence possibly a high take up rate would follow.

The particular consultancy has considerable experience on this kind of work and in fact has been correct in its assessment of future markets on 80% of its past contracts.

We now have all the elements we need to complete our probability calculations.

We have:

P(H) — the probability of a high take up rate
P(L) — the probabability of a low take up rate

these are:

P(H) = 0.9
P(L) = 0.1

What we want to find is:

P(H/F) — the probability of a high take up rate, given the consultants make a favourable report.

We know from our earlier work on the coin tossing that this probability, P(H/F) is found as follows:

$$P(H/F) = \frac{P(H)P(F/H)}{P(H)P(F/H) + P(L)P(F/L)}$$

We have P(H) and P(L), we need P(F/H) and P(F/L) to solve the equation.

P(F/H) is the probability that the consultants report is favourable given that there is eventually a high take up rate. This is the measure of accuracy of the consultant. It is similar to the probability of the expert predicting a head given that a head eventually lands face up. P(F/H) in this current example is 0.8 as the consultants have been correct 80% of the time.

P(F/L) is the probability that the consultants report is favourable given that there is a low take up. In other words the report said that the take up would be high but the take up was in fact low. This must be 0.2 the 20% of the time their prediction is not accurate.

We can now solve the equation for P(H/F).

$$P(H/F) = \frac{(0.9)(0.8)}{(0.9)(0.8) + (0.1)(0.2)}$$
$$= \frac{0.72}{0.74}$$
$$= 0.97$$

The corresponding calculations for P(L/F) would be:

$$P(L/F) = \frac{P(L)P(F/L)}{(P(L)P(F/L) + P(H)P(F/H)}$$
$$= \frac{(0.1)(0.2)}{(0.1)(0.2) + (0.9)(0.8)}$$
$$= \frac{0.02}{0.74}$$
$$= 0.03$$

And so the revised or posterior probability of there being a high take up rate is 0.97. We are now 97% sure that the take up rate will be high *if* the consultant reports that it will be high.

In Fig. 5.8 (overleaf) we have drawn a revised tree for our problem because now we must decide whether or not to employ the consultant, in other words we have to decide on the value of the information we may get from him.

This new tree shows the new decision situation. The only probabilities we have not mentioned yet are the probabilities associated with outcomes of the consultant's report. The report may be favourable or unfavourable and the tree shows these figures as:

$$P(F) = 0.74$$
$$P(UF) = 0.26$$

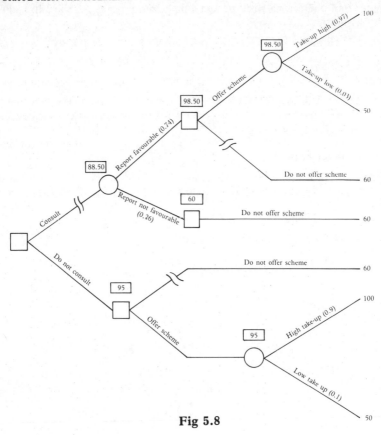

Fig 5.8

The figure 0.74 comes from the denominator of the Bayes formula and represents the two ways in which a report may be favourable i.e., it may be favourable and the take up rate is high or it may be favourable and the take up is low.

When the tree is averaged out and we roll back the information we are led to the decision not to engage the consult. The EMV of consulting is £88.50 compared to an EMV of £95 from not consulting. This takes no account of the cost of obtaining the consultants information and so if this cost was £2 we would be comparing £86.50 with £95.

Let us be clear what we have done. We have revised our initial probability in the light of a report which itself may be right or wrong. The consultant's report is only a prediction and we have taken the accuracy of his previous predictions into account in revising our initial probability. There seems to be no value in the additional information at all. This is in contrast to the previous example with the coin testing. Can you think of a difference between that illustration and this one which has made a difference?

The reason the value of the information in the coin tossing was high is due to the initial probability only being 0.5. We were just as likely to select a head as a tail and so almost any additional information would help. In the current illustration we are already 90% sure of a high take up, even before engaging a consultant.

5.5   Applying Bayesian Analysis to the Basic Decision

Let us return now to the problem of reducing the level of shrinkage. If you turn back to Fig.5.3 you will see the last decision tree we drew for the problem. At that time we were considering a redesign of the store which made our risk reduction mechanisms more effective. Net savings increased by 50% and even although the redesign was to cost £5,000 we decided to do it.

You will recall from that tree that the risk manager estimated that the redesign would be successful in reducing shrinkage, with a probability of 0.8. Let us say now that he would like some independent review of the whole matter and have contacted a firm of security consultants. For a fee, they will review the new design of the store and consider the various possible outcomes. This particular firm has considerable experience in dealing with similar matters and in fact has correctly forecast that store redesigns would reduce shrinkage with an 85% level of accuracy. Their accuracy in correctly predicting that a redesign would not reduce shrinkage is 70%.

Here again we have all the classic elements of a Bayesian calculation,

- we have a prior probability
- we have access to new information
- we can calculate a posterior probability

In this example we have:

- the prior probability of the redesign being successful
- this is 0.8. We will refer to this as P(R).
  The prior probability that the redesign will be unsuccessful is $P(\overline{R})$ or 0.2.
- the new information we have is the advice of the consultants. They will either say that the redesign will be successful, P(C) or that it will be unsuccessful $P(\overline{C})$.
  They can, of course, be right or wrong in their advice and the only measure we have of their accuracy is their past record.
  The probability of them saying the redesign will be successful and it is in fact successful P(C/R), is 0.85. This is the 85% accuracy figure we mentioned above.
  The probability of them saying the redesign will be unsuccessful and it turns out to be unsuccessful $P(\overline{C}/\overline{R})$ is 0.70. We can see, therefore, that their record in predicting success is better than predicting failure. (This is a little different from the earlier two illustrations we used. In these illustrations we assumed that the chance of the expert producing a favourable report was the same regardless of whether he was predicting success or failure. In the case of the expert who commented on the chance of a high or low take up of the insurance scheme, used in the earlier example, we saw that his success rate was 80% whether this was in predicting a high take up or a low take up rate).
- what we want to calculate is the probability that the shrinkage will reduce given that the consultant says it will reduce, P(R/C). We may also want to

calculate the probability that shrinkage will reduce given that the consultant says it will not $P(R/\overline{C})$.

We are now ready to draw the new tree for this expanded decision and feed in all the new probabilities. Just before doing that, let us note down the probabilities we have at the moment.

$P(R)$ = Probability of shrinkage reducing = (0.8)
$P(\overline{R})$ = Probability that shrinkage will not reduce = (0.2)
$P(C/R)$ = Probability of the consultant saying shrinkage will reduce given that it does reduce = (0.85)
$P(\overline{C}/R)$ = Probability of the consultant saying shrinkage will not reduce given that shrinkage does in fact reduce.
(these two events, $P(C/R)$ and $P(\overline{C}/R)$, are opposites of each other i.e., either the consultant says shrinkage will reduce and it does *or* he says it will not reduce and it does in fact reduce). (0.15).
$P(\overline{C}/\overline{R})$ = the probability that the consultant says shrinkage will not reduce, given that it does not in fact reduce = (0.70)
$P(C/\overline{R})$ = the probability that the consultant says shrinkage will reduce given that it does not reduce i.e., he inaccurately forecasts the fact that shrinkage does not reduce = (0.30).

We have drawn the new tree — Fig. 5.9. (opposite).

Now we can see the new structure of the decision. Starting from the left we are faced with three possible alternatives, we can consult the security consultancy, redesign the store layout or not redesign the layout.

Should we employ the consultancy then their report may either say that shrinkage will not reduce as a result of the new layout. Regardless of what the consultant says you are then faced with the decision of whether to redesign or not, and so on to the tips of the tree.

The outcome at the tips of the branches are those which we saw already in Fig.5.3. These have been averaged out at the first chance node and then the alternative yielding the highest EMV has been selected. If we employed the consultant, the report said that shrinkage would fall *and* we redesigned we are then at a chance node. Shrinkage may now either fall or rise and down each path we see the EMV's of £20.7 and £13.8 respectively. (All the figures have been expressed as 000's to avoid all the zeros in the trees and the calculations). At the end of the branch which represents a fall we have £20.7 and at the end of the branch which represents a rise we have £13.8. You can see the probability of these two branches occurring is 0.92 and 0.08 respectively. These were calculated using the Bayesian formula we have already illustrated.

The chance of shrinkage falling, given that the consultant said it would, is the branch which has £20.7 at the end. In probabilistic language this is $P(R/C)$. By referring back to the earlier illustrations of the Bayesian calculation we can see that:

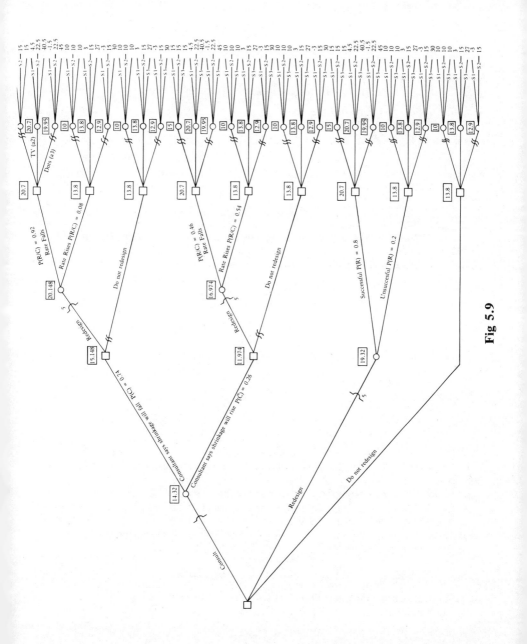

Fig 5.9

$$P(R/C) = \frac{P(R)P(C/R)}{P(R)P(C/R) + P(\overline{R})P(C/\overline{R})}$$

$$= \frac{(0.8)(0.85)}{(0.8)(0.85) + (0.2)(0.3)}$$

$$= \frac{0.68}{0.74}$$

$$= 0.92$$

$P(\overline{R}/C)$ is therefore $(1 - 0.92) = 0.08$

Using these two probabilities and averaging out, we get an expected monetary value of £20.14 above the relevant chance node. And so if the consultant says the store redesign will reduce shrinkage then we can either redesign or not.

The EMV of redesigning is £20.148 and if not doing so is £13.8. With these figures we would block off the "don't redesign road" and go for the redesign.

If the consultant says the rate of shrinkage will not reduce then we are faced with the same decision, will we redesign or not. To answer this question we must find the probability of shrinkage reducing, given that the consultant says it will not reduce, $P(R/\overline{C})$. We also see the opposite of this, $P(\overline{R}/\overline{C})$ which is the probability that shrinkage will not fall, given that the consultant says it will not fall.

In terms of the Bayesian formula, we need firstly:

$$P(R/\overline{C}) = \frac{P(R)P(\overline{C}/R)}{P(R)P(\overline{C}/R) + P(\overline{R})P(\overline{C}/\overline{R})}$$

$$= \frac{(0.8)(0.15)}{(0.8)(0.15)+(0.2)(0.7)}$$

$$= \frac{0.12}{0.26}$$

$$= 0.46$$

$P(\overline{R}/\overline{C})$ is therefore $(1- 0.46)$ or 0.54

We can now average out and roll back. We can see that if we move down the branch corresponding to the choice of consultant, then we are faced with a chance node, either the consultant says that shrinkage will rise or that it will fall. At the end of the two branches corresponding to these chance events we have two EMV's of £15.148 and £11.974. We don't know which one of these will occur and so we have to average out once again. We therefore need to find the probability that the consultant will say shrinkage is going to fall. We have shown this as P(C). The probability that he says shrinkage will not fall is $P(\overline{C})$.

Let us concentrate on P(C) the probability that he says shrinkage will fall. This can only come about in one of two ways, either shrinkage falls and he said it would fall or shrinkage does not fall and he said it would fall. In probabilistic terms this would be:

$$P(R \text{ and } C) \text{ or } P(\overline{R} \text{ and } C)$$

Alternative events like this are added together to get the probability of the alternative event and so:

$$P(C) = P(R \text{ and } C) + P(\overline{R} \text{ and } C)$$

We know from our knowledge of probabilities that joint events are multiplied to get the joint probability and so we can extend the above to:

$$P(C) = P(R)P(C/R) + P(\overline{R})P(C/\overline{R})$$

When we look back at the various formulae we have already used we see that $P(R)P(C/R) + P(\overline{R})P(C/\overline{R})$ is in fact the denominator of the formula used to find $P(R/C)$. It was in fact 0.74.

(We have already seen this idea in earlier examples when we calculated $P(F)$ and $P(UF)$ in the example of the extended service being offered to employees and in calculating $P(SH)$ and $P(ST)$ when the expert was predicting heads or tails).

All we need now is $P(\overline{C})$ to complete the probabilities. $P(\overline{C})$ is the denominator of the formula used to obtain $P(R/\overline{C})$. (See if you can prove this yourself). It is in fact 0.26.

Notice that $P(C)$ and $P(\overline{C})$ sum to one. They must do as they are mutually exclusive events which are also exhaustive of all possibilities.

When we average out the chance of the consultant giving a favourable or unfavourable report we find an EMV of £14.32, this compares to an EMV of £19.32 if we go ahead and redesign immediately and an EMV of £13.80 if we don't redesign.

We have three EMV's:

Alternative	£ EMV
Consult the expert	14.32
Redesign	19.32
Don't redesign	13.80

The tree in Fig.5.9 has been useful in that it has allowed us to calculate all the probabilities for the Bayesian revision of the prior probabilities. However, it is rather unrealistic in the sense that we have not really acted on the outcome of the consultants advice. The tree shows that regardless of what the consultant says, we will go through the same decision process. As a result, the EMV's for consulting and not consulting are identical at £14.32

In any real situation we would of course be looking at the consequences of acting on advice, as we did in the tree in Fig.5.8.

5.6   Conclusion

We have come a very long way in the space of a couple of chapters! What we have included is all fairly standard material in most texts on management or business decision making. It may have seemed a lot, especially to those who find working with numbers rather strange. However risk managers must arm themselves with the kind of tools other managers have at their disposal.

It is not suggested for a moment that you will carry out this kind of analysis every week of the year or indeed report the findings of this quantitive analysis in a quantitive way. Used properly these tools are an aid to decision making. They do not take decisions for you but they can allow you to evaluate alternatives and develop a structured approach to solving problems.

Those wishing to read another text on the material covered in the previous chapters on decision analysis may find the book "Anatomy of Decisions" by Hull, Moore and Thomas useful. It is published in Paperback form by Penguin and is reasonably priced.

Chapter 6

FORECASTING IN RISK MANAGEMENT

6.1   Introduction

The decision making process all too often is based upon subjectivity. Resolution of problems have been the result of hunches and rules of thumb. Intuition has been the norm. That is not say that intuitive decision making is bad, for there are many instances where 'gut' feelings cover many of the factors affecting a business enterprise and hence problem resolution has been reasonably successful. This is particularly so in the successful small business where management have a wider knowledge of those factors which can be controlled. However, as businesses grow and control becomes more widely disseminated among members of a much larger management team, intuitive decision making (such as forecasting future performance) becomes more difficult. For this reason it seems reasonable to suggest that something is required which will supplement such forecasting; something that will provide a sound yet more educated basis for forecasting the future. If this were possible, then risk managers may be able to make more effective decisions and possibly minimise the effects of wrong judgements.

But why should risk managers bother using more effective forecasting techniques? The answer is simple. We live in an environment of change; new technology, new disciplines (such as Risk Management itself), changes in Government policies, increased international trade and importantly the need to maintain the 'competitive edge' all add to the need for more timely and more effective decision making. For those reasons, the decision maker is better off understanding some of the quantitative forecasting techniques and using them wisely rather than carrying out plans in ignorance of supplementary information which may be available. There are four identifiable reasons for using forecasting, namely:-

(i)   It provides a more sound basis for decision making.

(ii) Actual figures are given, therefore there is a base for establishing budgets. That this is so allows a comparison of expectations with actual performance to be made. This, in turn, facilitates remedial action should it be necessary.

(iii) Indications are given as to the possible effects upon expectations given changes in chosen environmental factors.

(iv) The Risk Manager is seen to present his forecasts in the same manner and style as other managers within the Company.

Fortunately there are techniques available which take decision making beyond a simple judgemental level and which will help a risk manager to resolve many of the problems that are laid before him. For example:-

(i)   A risk manager may wish to know how shrinkage might be affected by changes in departmental staffing levels.

(ii) Management may be concerned at the variability in work injury rates at a number of their factories. Some may be particularly good, others particularly poor. Forecasting techniques may help to identify those factors that may discriminate that variability and thereby provide initiatives that may help to improve future performance.

(iii) A local authority may be anxious to set its domestic rate tariff. Their risk manager is asked to provide more accurate budgets. He is worried at his inability to predict future accidents caused by the authority's bus fleet. Forecasting techniques will help to resolve this perceived difficulty.

(iv) The corporate accountant at a chemical plant wishes to know what provisions he should make for the following three years against possible losses arising from atmospheric pollution. Forecasting techniques would be a valuable aid to the risk manager in assessing what these provisions should be.

These, are but a few examples of the problems which may face a risk manager; problems which require to be resolved. Though not a perfect panacea for success, the use of proper forecasting techniques will help the risk manager resolve these issues with greater confidence thereby assisting corporate management in their forward planning.

6.2   A Framework for Corporate Forecasting

Let us for a moment consider the framework within which forecasting is made.

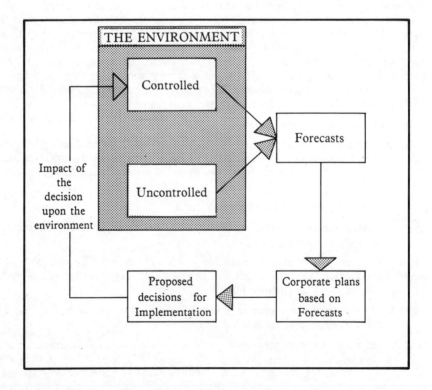

Figure 6.1: A Forecasting Framework

Figure 6.1 serves to express a model relationship between forecasting and the environment within which an organisation operates. As will be seen there are, in this model, two elements to the environment. The first, controlled; in other words that element of the environment which the organisation can manipulate. This would include, for example, cost of risk allocations. The second is an element over which an organisation has little, if any, control, namely the 'uncontrolled environment'. It includes, for example, the consequences of government action or of their fiscal policies: perhaps even the consequences of changes in consumer preferences or public attitudes. Clearly these have a bearing upon corporate plans and effective forecasting will ensure that proposed decisions which are made make those plans achieveable with greater confidence.

Such decisions, once made, themselves cause change. The model is never static. It is in a perpetual state of movement.

6.2   A Typology of Forecasts

Forecasting techniques do vary according to whether the need is long (or short) term; is summary (or detail) or whatever the need may be satisfied by qualitative (rather than quantitative) statements.

6.3.1   The Time Horizon

It is perhaps apposite at this juncture to put forecasting into the context of an organisational heirarchy such as is represented in figure 6.2.

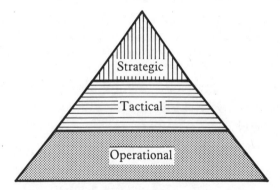

Figure 6.2. The Decision Making Structure of an Organisation

Figure 6.2 indicates, in diagrammatic form, the decision making structure of most organisations. At the top there are those decisions which set organisational policy and direction. Here are found the strategy makers whose time frame is long term in its nature. They rarely consider matters much less than two years in advance; more frequently well beyond that. Forecasts may have to provide support for a course of action that spreads over many years. In other words they are strategic in their context.

Below that is middle management whose concern is with maintaining tactics in such a fashion that strategy is attained. Here, the time-frame is shorter and hence forecasts must be able to support decisions that operate within a 6-month to two year period.

At the bottom level is to be found operations; in other words those functions that cover the day-to-day routines. Here the time-frame is more-or-less immediate and forecasts that are provided must be able to support operational needs; response must be quick if adequate controls are to be carried out. Operationally, quick decisions may be needed, particularly if the business is operating in a volatile pattern. Any such forecasting mechanism must, in the light of any consequent modification, implicit in our earlier discussions on environmental changes, be able to respond quickly.

6.3.2   The Level of Detail

This classification concerns itself with how 'particular' the data is. At one extreme, detailed, at the other summary. The former (micro) would include, for example, a forecast that centres upon the expected shrinkage losses from a particular product line say at one branch of a retail organisation. In such an instance actual recorded daily losses may be the basis for a 'local' forecast.

The latter (macro) is more concerned with large summary values; for example expected overall shrinkage may be based upon a series of averages extracted from a variety of product lines over all branches.

6.3.3   Qualitative or Quantitative?

The third classification differentiates qualitative forecasting (that is forecasts where there is no overt data manipulation and is purely judgemental) from quantitative (which at its extreme is entirely data based and requires no judgemental input whatsoever). Clearly, however there is the middle line, namely those decisions which are partly both.

Such categorisation clearly opens up a number of questions among them:-

(i) How specific must the detail be?

(ii) How quickly is the forecast required?

(iii) To what extent are qualitative/quantitative factors appropriate?

These must be answered for the choice of specific techniques depends much upon the response made.

6.4   The Structuring of Forecasting

The function of forecasting is clearly the projection of past data and experiences into an uncertain future. There are four basic steps in the process namely data collection, data reduction and condensation, model building and model extrapolation. This is summarised in figure 6.3. (opposite).

It is within such a framework that the risk manager should manage his postulations. Forecasting, if it is to be objective and made with confidence, must be carried out in a rigorous and effective manner. Taking a holistic view, it is but a small contribution to decision making. However it is important for it takes

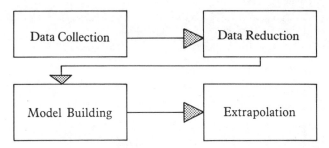

Figure 6.3: The Forecasting Process

decision making beyond the boundaries of pure judgement and adds confidence to judgements made.

6.5   Correlation

Let us now turn to the first stage in forecasting by considering relationships that exist between different variables. Risk managers should not underestimate the value of correlation procedures for they provide a basis of answering questions raised concerning the relationship of one variable with another. There are a variety of correlation techniques available. Specifically we will deal with Pearson's Coefficient, Auto Correlation and the Spearman Rank Coefficient.

Turning to correlation and the relationship that exists between two different random variables, we see that a random variable is some quantitative observation whose specific values vary from case to case or from trial to trial; such variations being on a chance basis.

6.5.1   Scattergraphs

Let us first examine the relationship between two variables which, for the time being, we will term X and Y. The nature of the relationship between such variables may be visually assessed by graphical representation. Such a graph is called a scattergraph or scatter diagram. For example we see in figure 6.4. (overleaf) that as the X variable rises, the Y variable does also.

The relationship is said to be perfect. Why? It is because as X increases so does Y and in a perfectly predictable manner. After all they do seem to lie in a perfect line, hence the description, a **perfect, positive, linear** relationship.

Let us put this into context. If, for example, our Y variable was the number of children in a family and the X variable represented the number of chimney pots on the roofs, then observation may tend to suggest a radical measure in the control of a population explosion. Clearly, such a conclusion is dangerous on a number of grounds. First, the sample size is very small (n=6) and second such a relationship is spurious.

97

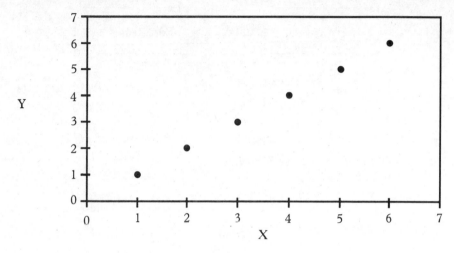

Figure 6.4: A Perfect, Positive, Linear Relationship

Let us now consider another scattergraph as in figure 6.5:-

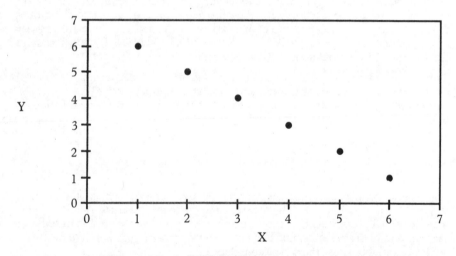

Figure 6.5: A Perfect, Negative, Linear Relationship

In this instance, the converse appears to be the case. In other words as X increases; Y decreases. Again, the plotted points appear to lie in a straight line. In such an instance we have a **perfect, negative, linear** relationship.

Further relationships between sets of data are possible. There are many instances where scattergraphs like those found in figures 6.6 and 6.7 are to be found. The former serves to illustrate a **curvi-linear** relationship; in other words, it is possible to suggest a relationship but it is one that clearly is not best explained by a straight line.

In the latter, the data is indicative of an absence of any linear relationship.

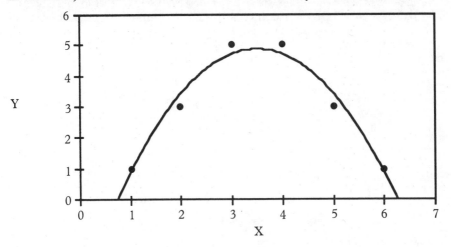

Figure 6.6: A Curvi-Linear Relationship

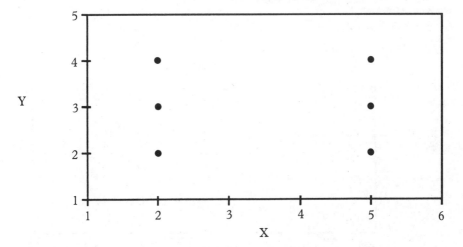

Figure 6.7: No Relationship

What is evident is that in considering any two variables, differing relationships between them arise and one way of obtaining a feel of the data is to draw such diagrams. Two simple examples will place the function of correlation in context.

Let us suppose that sets of two measurements have been taken. For example, we might measure the level of loss-contingency funds for a number of corporate bodies and the rate of return that each fund receives; we might determine the income of a number of risk managers and their age and then ask ourselves for each set "what is the nature of the relationship between the two variables we have measured?"

Let us assume that the following figures represent the findings from our investigations. Set A identifies six pairs of observations. Observation 1 shows a 10% rate of return (ROR) is associated with a £4.4m contingency fund; the second, 7% with a £4.5m contingency and so on. The second set of data, though independent of the first, takes the same format. Notice that a 27 year old risk manager enjoys an income of £30,000 (observation 6) and a 24 year old, £40,000 (observation 4).

	Set A		Set B	
ROR		£m	Inc (£ 000's)	Age
10		4.4	15	34
7		4.5	25	35
3		3.7	50	27
6		3.4	40	24
8		4.3	20	33
5		3.7	30	27

Figure 6.8

What then is the case with the data set out in Figure 6.8. In both these instances, we see that the data does not really fall into any of the categories outlined above yet clearly there is an underlying trend:-

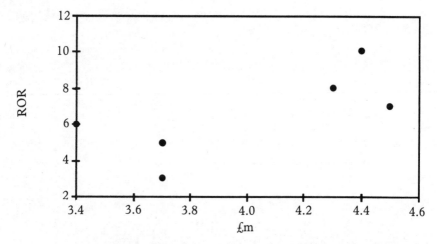

Figure 6.9: An Imperfect, Positive Relationship ›

Figure 6.9, our scattergraph, shows that as our investment level increases there is a tendency for the rate of return to be higher. A perfect relationship? Not quite, but it is an **imperfect, positive** relationship.

What then of the earning capacity of risk managers? What is the nature of the relationship between their age and their income. Again, a scattergraph will help:-

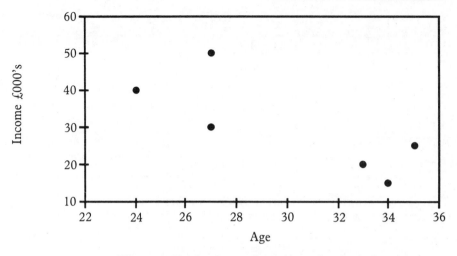

Figure 6.10: An Imperfect, Negative Relationship

Simple observation indicates that the older risk managers seems to earn less and hence the data suggests an **imperfect, negative** relationship.

In conclusion, it is clear that when we consider two variables, mere plotting of the data will give us a feeling of the nature of the relationship between them. In some instances a perfect linear relationship is self-evident (figures 6.4 and 6.5). If we were to fit a line through these points and establish a mathematical equation that describes that line, then we would have a model which for any value of X would produce a value of Y.

In others, a straight line seems best if not perfect (figures 6.9 and 6.10) and if we were able to establish that line, we could use it for the purposes of prediction. The question is this, given that a straight line can be fitted, what is the degree of the relationship that exists between the two variables under consideration?

Correlation provides such a measure.

6.5.2   Pearson's Coefficient of Correlation (r)

In investigating two variables a measure of the closeness of the relationship between them lies in the concept of correlation. We have already discussed the nature of a variety of possible relationships and Pearson's product-moment Coefficient of Correlation (represented by 'r') provides one measure of the strength of that linear relationship.

If the linear relationship is perfectly positive then r = +1.0. If perfectly negative then r = -1.0. As these values tend to zero so does the weakness of the correlation. It will be seen that there are two aspects to the coefficient. First its sign (which indicates whether an increase in Y is linearly associated with either an increase in X or with a decrease in X and second its value; a measure of strength.

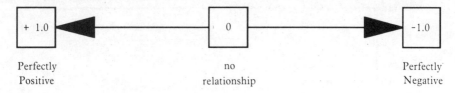

Perfectly	no	Perfectly
Positive	relationship	Negative

Figure 6.11: The Strength and Sign of r

Thus, we have:-

r·	The Relationship
r = +1.0	Perfect Positive Linear.
r = —1.0	Perfect Negative Linear.
r = +1<0	Imperfect Positive Relationship.
r = —1>0	Imperfect Negative Relationship.
r = 0	No relationship.

Clearly, if we are able to establish the value of **r** from our data we can obtain a measure of the degree to which the points are linearly related. If the data dispersion is low, then it seems reasonable to conclude that there is a close association between the two variables. If the disperson is large then the relationship is weak and any predictions that we make may be subject to large error. The reader need not worry too much about these procedures for fortunately now there are many computer packages available that do all this work for you.

6.5.3   Problems in Interpretating

There exist a number of traps when one is considering the interpretation of **r**. First, simply because **r** is low does not mean to say that there is no relationship (it could be that the relationship is curvilinear). In addition, it is possible that another variable could affect the relationship. This is a matter of multicolinearity (an aspect we will turn to later).

Also, we must watch out for spurious data. For example, correlations have been found between sunspot activity and car production, skirt lengths and the rabbit population. There may exist a high correlation between the number of grouse shot on Rannoch Moor and 'fatality settlements' under an insurance company's employers liability portfolio. Clearly there is no causal connection; the association is accidental; it is spurious. Cause and effect must be considered and this can only happen when there exists the essential background information.

6.5.4   Autocorrelation

A special situation is to be found when we are interested in measuring the extent to which a variable is correlated with itself when lagged over a period of time. Where we are concerned with such a relationship, in other words a type of self-correlation, then it is called autocorrelation.

Resultant values of **r** give an indication of the extent to which the data are correlated with themselves, and it is particularly appropriate when developing a time series model! We will return to this matter later.

6.5.5   Spearman's Rank Correlation (r_s)

The correlation discussed so far has been 'Pearsonian' in its nature. There is another correlation coefficient which measures the extent to which two sets of <u>ranked</u> data are related to each other. This measure is known as Spearmans Rank Correlation Coefficient and is normally represented, r_s. Again, it is possible to carry out analyses on computers and the interpretation of findings is as considered earlier except in this instance any discussion on the relationship must be limited to between ranks.

6.5.6   A Concluding Word on Correlation

Risk managers may often wish to know the nature of the relationship that exists between much of the data that they have. For example, they may wish to know whether poor productivity levels are associated with absence rates, income or health or safety training. The frequency of minor accidents might be associated with hours of overtime; inventory levels may be related to theft or cash flow. These are but a few examples of appropriate applications for correlation theory; a theory which is a very potent tool for measuring the degree of linear association between any two variables.

The reader must be clear that correlation is but one of the many types of statistical tests that are available and an understanding of correlation is a critical pre-requisite to interpretation in the techniques that will follow; correlation is central to regression analysis (simple and multiple) and to time series.

6.6   Simple Regression

We shall now deal with the two types of regression, namely:-

(i) Simple regression

(ii) Multiple regression

The main objective of many forecasting techniques is to establish relationships which make it possible to predict one or more variables in terms of others. Let us continue with the shrinkage debate where we assumed that a risk manager of a large retail organisation was concerned at the level of shrinkage losses that have been occurring. The risk manager now has a 'gut feeling' that one possible explanation lies in the relatively low wages being paid; staff members feel that they have a 'right' to pilfer.

Within the context of this example it would be most useful for the risk manager to be able to predict the extent of future losses, particularly the expected savings from the implementation of a potential risk management programme? Would it not be better that the risk manager makes his decisions based upon the knowledge that if there is one set of quantities that he can control then another set of quantities could be predicted with near certainty? The risk manager will surely realise that the predicting ability of one quantity (such as future losses) vis-a-vis another (for example, salary levels) could assist his decision making to become much more effective particularly if weight is given to the predicting ability of that relationship.

This problem of predicting the value of one variable from another is one that is resolved by the process of regression. Regression is a technique which establishes the relationship between variables but which does not measure its strength. This latter aspect, of course, is a matter for correlation, a concept which we covered earlier. Regression then, (to consider this example) is concerned with predicting what might be the average level of losses given some suitable data with which it can be compared. The reader should note the use of the term average. As a process, regression will not predict what a loss will be,

Risk management decision making is a complex process and the reality of loss management (to use the example already cited) is that shrinkage is likely to be affected by more than just poor wage levels. Other factors too may be contributing. Such factors as the frequency of delivery schedules, product scarcity, black market availability and the extent of peer pressure come to mind. This latter aspect, namely the prediction of losses from a number of other factors, is matter for what is known as multiple regression an aspect to which we will turn later. In the meantime, however, we will make an assumption, namely that there is only one 'affecting' variable involved. This, of course, is an assumption that is generally invalid but we will maintain it in order to demonstrate the principles of simple regression.

6.6.1   Building a Simple Regression Model

We have already seen how the relationship between two sets of variables may be diagrammatically represented by using a scattergraph. In figure 6.12, we repeat the content of figures 6.4 and 6.5. It will be recalled that these showed a perfect positive and a perfect negative relationship between two sets of data represented by X and Y. The nature of these variables is not important but it is clear in both instances that the co-ordinates can all be joined together by a straight line, a line which can be represented mathematically by the general formula $y = a + bx$.

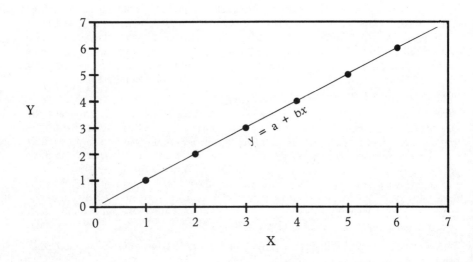

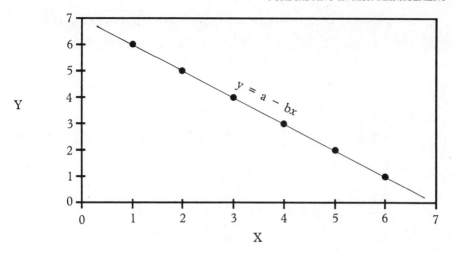

$$y = a - bx$$

Figure 6.12: Linearily Related Variables

Now imagine that you are the risk manager for a large multinational organisation in which there exists a certain homogenous risk. You take a random sample of 10 industrial units throughout your organisation. The following data represents the results of your investigation. The first column provides a measure of the risk, namely the **Annual Rate of Injury** at each of these ten locations and the **Annual Rate of Absence** from safety meetings you arranged. Your rationale for taking these measures is your feeling that high rates of injury are associated with high absence rates from safety meetings.

Annual Rate of Injury at Work	Annual Rate of Absence from Safety Meetings
3	20
1	18
4	27
2	21
4	17
4	24
4	21
3	21
3	22
2	19

First our visual presentation, namely the scattergraph. Figure 6.13 identifies in the relationship between the two variables.

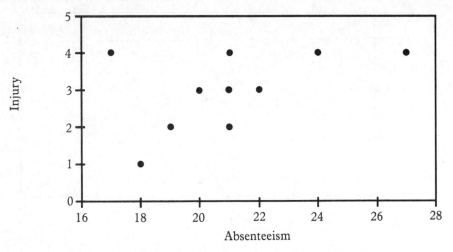

Figure 6.13: Scattergraph of Annual Rate of Injury with Absenteeism

What then is the correlation between them? Relying upon our computer programme and without going into the mathematics of the procedure, we find that $r = +0.472$. This is not very high but it does suggest there to be a positive linear relationship between the data. On this basis we might progress with developing our predicting model and in any analysis, it is important to decide what is the best predicting equation. There are many methods of determining the equation. For our purposes we will limit our consideration to that of a linear relationship and the derivation of the linear equation; an equation which is perhaps the most widely used forecasting technique.

6.6.2   The Regression Line

It is clear from figure 6.13 that the data of this example does not boast a perfect linear relationship but the reader will realise that a line could be fitted. The question is; of those shown in figure 6.14, (opposite) which is best; is it (a) or (b) or (c)?

Consider (a). This lies through the co-ordinates (1,18) and (4,27). The only other co-ordinate that this line 'satisfies' is (2,21). The line satisfies none other. Similar comments can be made concerning lines (b) and (c). In fact of the infinite number of possible lines there is not one line that will satisfy all co-ordinates. Nevertheless there is one that is <u>the best</u> line, the problem is which one! By using a technique of least squares, that line is identified. In effect, the technique considers all the data and establishes a line such that the total deviations of the data from that line is reduced to a minimum; at best to zero and at second best as near to zero as possible. Clearly, it will not be possible to reduce the deviations in this example to zero for here there will always be some co-ordinates that lie off the line.

The resultant equation is known as the regression equation; it is the equation of the mean line or the average line and is that equation which will act as a basis for providing the best prediction of the annual rate of injury given the knowledge of absenteeism (a variable which the risk manager feels he can control).

Figure 6.15 superimposes the regression line upon the scattergraph.

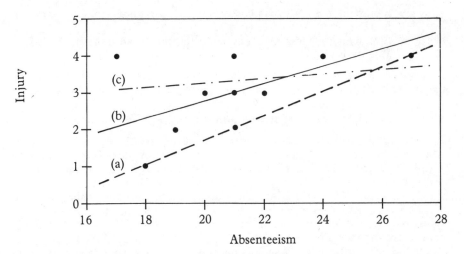

Figure 6.14: Three Possible Lines to Fit the Data

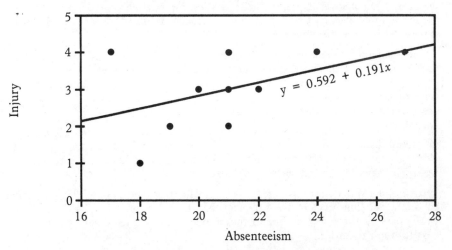

Figure 6.15: The Data with the Regression Line Drawn

It will be observed that the line has a positive slope (ie as x increases so does y). This, of course, is in keeping with our knowledge of the coefficient of correlation.

The equation, in this instance turns out to be y = 0.592 + 0.191 *(x)* which may be represented in a more 'general' form namely:-

where:-

    Y represents the dependent variable (in this example the annual rate of injury)

    a represents the constant term (ie the value of y where x = 0), in this instance 0.592

      b   represents the regression coefficient. (i.e. the slope of the line), here it is 0.191

and   **x**   represents the independent variable. (in this instance the annual rate of absenteeism)

It is worth noting that where Pearson's coefficient of correlation is positive, the regression coefficient is too. Similarly, if it is negative then b will be negative.

6.6.3   Some Words of Warning about Simple Regression

In this example we have centred upon deriving the simple regression equation which can be used to estimate y (the annual rate of injury) from a given value of x (the annual rate of absenteeism). For example, you might be interested in predicting the rate of injury given an absence rate of 19 or, say, 25. We would simply substitute these values into the equation and obtain our predicted values, say 2.657 and 3.683 respectively. The reader will note that the two suggested values of x are within the range of the available data (as will be seen from figure 6.12 where the maximum value is 27 and the minimum value is 17). This raises doubt concerning the value of such a model in predicting y, when chosen values of the independent variable lie outside the given range. Clearly, there is danger for we do not know what happens to the relationship between the variables beyond the extremities of what we know to be the case. It is therefore inadvisable to use the model in such circumstances.

There is another danger area. In this instance, we have regressed y on x, not x on y. In other words, the reader must not assume that once a regression equation has been established that it can equally be used to predict x from y. In other words, this equation is NOT a valid model to use if you were interested in predicting absenteeism from the rate of injury.

Additionally, the reader must be sure to realise that we do not provide an exact prediction using the regression equation. An example will help to make this clear. If we return to our set of known figures, for example the first observation (3,20), we might have 'estimated' **y** from **x**, thus y = -0.592 + 1.71 (20) = 2.828.

That 2.828 results, rather than 3 is not a failing on the part of the regression equation; but simply a feature of the fact that the line is one of "best fit" and that whilst passing through a couple of the points on the scatter diagram it does not pass through them all.

6.7   The Coefficients of Determination and of Alienation

We mentioned earlier that Pearson's Coefficient of Correlation was +0.472. It is appropriate now to consider two further measures. First the coefficient of determination (represented by r^2), a measure which indicates how much of the variability in a dependent variable is explained by the relationship with the independent variable. In this instance the coefficient of determination is approximately 0.22; in other words 22% of the variable in the rate of injury at work is explained by the relationship between rates of injury and attendance at safety meetings. Let us now consider the other side of the coin. If 22% is explained, 78% remains unexplained. This latter value, (ie $1-r^2$) is known as the coefficient of alienation and in this example it is really telling us that other variables are perhaps at work.

All these figures we have considered so far can be calculated using relevant software packages. On balance, despite what the data appears to show, the correlation coefficient is weak (healthy correlations are usually greater than $\pm$ 0.9) and the results do suggest that the role of the rate of absence from safety meetings as the sole independent variable is doubtful; it appears that our regression model is of little value for the purposes of controlling and predicting losses.

6.8   Multiple Regression

So far we have considered the process of simple regression. That is a process which concerns itself with one dependent and one independent variable. We have seen how such a process provides a means of estimating the effect on the first of the second. However real life is not that simple. More than one independent variable is usually necessary in order to predict a dependent variable accurately. When this is the case then the problem becomes one of multiple regression analysis which conceptually is little different from simple regression and is one to which we will now turn.

6.8.1   A Second Predicting Variable and the problem of Colinearity

Let us return to our example. We have already found out that the coefficient of correlation is +0.47 and that the coefficient of determination is 0.22. We saw that only 22% of the variablity in the rate of injury at work was explained by its relationship with the rate of absence from safety meetings and we concluded that the absence rate was not valuable on its own.

The question that remains open is this:-

"Is there another variable which may help to explain that which remains unexplained?"

What the risk manager needs to find is another predictor variable or variables; in other words another independent variable that is related more strongly to the rate of injury.

Let us for a moment consider another possible variable which could affect the rate of injury at work, namely the rate of overtime. As risk manager you extend your survey of the ten 'identical' units and come up with the following data:-

Annual Rate of Injury	Annual Rate of Absence	Annual Overtime Rate
3	20	20
1	18	20
4	27	30
2	21	21
4	17	38
4	24	39
4	21	41
3	21	30
3	22	31
2	19	20

Figure 6.16: Revised Schedule of Data

We don't yet know whether this additional information will help but we can pre-empt matters by investigating the nature of the relationship between the rate of injury and the rate of overtime (which we will accept as being expressed in hours per day). We can do this by calculating Pearsons Coefficient of Correlation. In this instance $r = +0.90$ ($r^2 = 0.81$). This tells you that you know 81% of what you need to know in order to estimate the rate of injury perfectly. We can now see that if we were to calculate the simple regression equation with the rate of overtime as the sole independent variable, then 19% remains unexplained.

What then of the combined effects? Will the effect of the overtime rate <u>and</u> the absence rate (both capable of being controlled by management) provide that much needed 'perfect' prediction.

At a glance you may be tempted to think that your problem has been solved for:-

| | (i) Absense explains | — 22% |
| and | (ii) Overtime explains | — 81% |

In total, 103% of the variability in the rate of absence, appears to be explained by the combined effects of these two independent variables! This just does not make sense. What then is wrong? The answer is simple. What has not been accounted for in that assumption is that the rate of absence and the level of overtime might themselves be related to each other. Clearly the extent of overtime work could have an effect upon attendance; the question that remains open concerns the extent of that relationship? Yet again correlation will provide an indication. In this instance $r = +0.23$ and hence even between the two variables that we have titled as 'independent' some of the variability in one is related to the other. In other words our independent variables are themselves not truly independent . . .. to be so, the correlation between them ought to be zero.

For a moment let us depart from our example and consider first, two independent variables A and B, variables which we will assume to be perfectly related to each other and second, a dependent variable, C. Clearly in considering the relationship of A with C, it will be possible to establish the extent of the variability in the latter that is explained by the former. Now consider B. As it is perfectly related to A, no additional explanation of the variability in C will be obtained. The additional of this second variable will not improve estimation. This is a problem of what is known as 'colinearity'. If this is the case the resolution is to avoid using such 'independent' variables together.

To summarise, the attributes of good predictor variables are:-

1. That they are related to the dependent variable.
2. That they are **NOT** related to each other. They are truly independent of one another.

Let us now return to our example. The various relationships between the variables we are considering may be represented in a matrix of correlations. Such a matrix is frequently produced by computer software:-

	Injury	Absenteeism	Overtime
Injury	1.000	—	—
Absenteeism	0.472	1.000	—
Overtime	0.904	0.230	1.000

Figure 6.17: Correlation Matrix

6.8.2   The Multiple Correlation Coefficient (R^2)

Let us interpret the correlations in figure 6.17. By considering the first column, we see that the correlation of 'overtime' with the 'rate of Injury' is higher than 'absence' is. The former will, therefore, be the better explanatory variable. We also see that 'overtime' and 'absence' are marginally related to each other ($r = +0.23$) thus there is a confounding effect between them, nevertheless by 'filtering out' that effect it is likely that we can provide some additional explanation of the rate of injury. Indeed, there is a measure known as the multiple correlation coefficient represented by R (note it is upper case to distinguish it from the lower case version, r which we know is the simple correlation coefficient). R is interpreted in much the same fashion as the simple correlation coefficient. In this instance R is $+0.944$; in other words 89% (R^2) of the variability in the dependent variable is explained by the combined effects of absence and overtime. The mathematics for the calcuation of R are rather heavy and will not be considered here but once obtained, the derivation of the multiple coefficient of determination and the multiple coefficient of alienation are straightforward. The latter is clearly 0.11. We may interpret R^2 by saying that where 81% of the variability in the rate of injury at work was explained by its relationship with the rate of overtime, by adding the absence rate into the calculations (and, of course, filtering out the combined effect of overtime and absence) an additional 8% (ie 0.89 - 0.81) of the variability in the rate of injury is now explained. Additionally, we can say that 11% remains unexplained by the combined effect of these two variables. Certainly it looks as though we are on the way to a perfect model and in the circumstances it is reasonable to establish the multiple regression equation.

Again the mathematics of deriving the multiple regression equation are beyond the needs of this text but our friendly computer is at our right (or perhaps left) hand and so we can readily establish the required equation as:-

$$y = -2.510 + 0.101x_1 + 0.113x_2$$

Note that there are two 'functions' of x. This is simply because our analysis is based upon two 'independent' variables.

Now let us try the equation's worth by 'estimating' known data. Again, let us estimate y (the rate of injury) using the first observation from figure 6.16, that is where the rate of absence (x_1 is 20 and overtime (x_2) is 29. In other words:-

$$y = -2.510 + 0.101 (20) + 0.113 (29) = 2.78$$

Again, this 'prediction' is not actually 3; that it is not, is simply a feature of the fact that there still remains a residual unexplained variation. A third 'independent' variable might complete the picture. However we will progress no further with this suggestion for the principles are the same. As with simple regression, we could choose any two values of the rate of absence and overtime rate and establish our expected rate of injury. For example, we might choose 23 and 21 as the possible values of x_1 and x_2; fit these into the equation and derive a predicted value of y, namely 1.883.

6.8.4   A Comment upon Multiple Regression

Multiple regression analysis is clearly an extension of the principle of simple regression analysis to the case where a dependent variable is related to a number of predictor variables. All the tests related to the simpler linear model are applicable to the multiple model and even the multiple correlation coefficient (**R**) and the multiple coefficient of determination (**R²**) have meanings similar to the simple correlation coefficient (**r**) and the simple coefficient of determination (**r²**).

The importance of the difference between these two models lies in their utility. There are very few risk management situations which may adequately rely upon simple regression whereas the multiple regression model (provided it is properly constructed) does . . . what? In general there can be a danger in 'over-fitting' and as a general rule of thumb the number of predictor variables should not be much more than four.

6.9   Time Series Analysis

Now let us turn to time series analysis. Here, the framework is much the same but in this instance the independent variable is time and the dependent variable (the variable which is under study) takes on different values over time. Whatever the variable that is being studied, if it is considered within the framework of chronological time periods (be it minutes or years) then the data is properly called a time series.

What then is the use of time series? Broadly speaking it is to analyse past patterns so that future business patterns may be predicted. Clearly, such analyses does not provide the perfect answer to the future but it is a most useful error-reducing technique.

There are many examples of data that can be dealt within the framework of time series analysis. The reader need only consult the maze of government statistics (for example, Social Trends and the Statistical Abstracts of the Central Statistical Office) to see appropriate examples. Within organisations, the monthly budgets, the annual reports and the many other documents that are prepared for internal consumption lend themselves to being analysed by this technique.

Time series, like regression analysis, does not boast of being an automatic recipe for success but it does make a useful contribution to reducing the uncertainty implicit in rational decision making.

6.9.1   The Components of a Time Series

The most common method of dealing with the anlayses of a time series is a procedure known as decomposition. Before turning to this aspect it is important to understand the underlying factors that have their effect upon each of the periodical values in a typical series of data. There are four:-

(i)   The Trend Component

This component (sometimes known as the secular trend, or moving average) is long-term in its nature and is evidenced by a regular, underlying movement. The trend characterises a gradual and persistent long-term decline or growth in a series.

(ii)   The Seasonal Component

This component comprises the 'seasonal' fluctuations that recur year after year in the same period and are found typically in data that is classified in a quarterly, monthly or weekly time frame wherein the fluctuations, more or less, have the same intensity.

Albeit most examples deal with variations within the framework of the seasons, the reader must realise that the term 'seasonal variation' is also applied to other inherently periodic movements in a series of data.

(iii) The Cyclical Component

There is this further component. Classically, it parallels the business cycle of prosperity, recession, depression and recovery which usually reflects changes in the economy caused by such factors as changes in wealth and social custom. For example, such a component is manifested in the world of insurance underwriting by the presence of 'hard' and 'soft' markets.

(iv) The Irregular Component

Finally, there are those fluctuations that are unpredictable and non-periodic. They are caused by special events such as strikes (for example, the Firemans' in 1972), wars (such as the Falklands War) and elections (as in 1987 & 1992).

6.9.2   Building the Time Series Model

To study the components of a time series, we must again do so within the framework of a mathematical model. Clearly, the actual data (which, as before, we will identify as Y), is a mathematical function of the various components we have discussed; in others words Y is a function of T (the trend), S (the seasonal variation, C (the cyclical variation) and R (the residual variation).

The question that remains open is what is the nature of the relationship?

Commonly, the nature of the model used shows the actual values in a time series as comprising either an 'additive' function of the components or a 'multiplicative' function. In other words:-

(i) $Y = T + S + C + R$ (The Additive Model)

or

(ii) $Y = T \cdot S \cdot C \cdot R$ (The Multiplicative Model)

Of course, where a component is not found (for example C and/or R) then it is simply dropped from the model.

6.9.3   Distinguishing the Models

How do we isolate the model we need to use? The answer is simple. The additive model is apposite to that set of circumstances (irrespective of the trend) where the oscillations in the data form a constant pattern. On the other hand, the multiplicative model is best used where there is a change in the oscillations. A couple of simple examples will help to make this clear.

If we consider the oscillations in figure 6.18, we see that, on balance, the amplitudes are fairly constant. There is no general tendency to increase or decrease. If we were to draw a line joining the peaks, and another joining the troughs, then these two lines would be nearly parallel. A Time Series analysis of the various levels of production would follow the **additive** model.

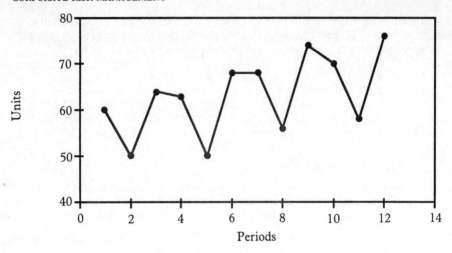

Figure 6.18: Graph of Production Series

What then of the multiplicative model? The graph shown in figure 6.19 shows the summer and winter average occupancies for an hypothetical hotel.

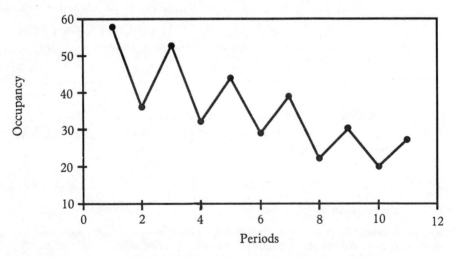

Figure 6.19: Series of Average Occupancy

Here, a general decline is clear but the oscillations are also diminishing; our lines joining the peaks and the troughs are not parallel. The appropriate model is **multiplicative.**

It will be seen that the choice of model is reasonably easy.

6.9.4   Decomposition of a Time Series

The secular trend to which we referred earlier provides an indication of the growth, stagnation or decline of a time series over the long term. It is the underlying smooth change; and is a descriptor of behaviour in the series. The goal of establishing this change is realised by using a process known as decomposition. This trend is more frequently referred to as the moving average.

The effect of decomposition is to remove the fluctuations in the original data but retain the underlying movement. This sort of procedure does produce a smoothing effect. Most standard text books on quantitative methods include descriptions of the mechanics of decomposition and the interested reader should seek such text should the fine detail of the method be of interest.

6.9.5   Establishing the Seasonal Variation

Thus we have it; a Time Series which contains a seasonal component and can comprise one of two models, the first, an additive model which we refined to $Y = T + S$ and a multiplicative model, refined to $Y = T \cdot S$. Given this, then it is clear that we can derive two possible equations for S namely $S = Y - T$ or $S = Y/T$ depending, of course, upon our choice of model. For the additive model, calculation of the seasonal variation is thereby a simple process of calculating the extent to which the Trend (T) deviates from the original data (Y). On the other hand, if we were to choose the multiplicative model the seasonal variation is the dividend of Y and T rather than the difference.

If the fluctuations in the data were regular, then the absolute value of the variations above the trend would equal the absolute value of variations below. However, random irregularities in the data frequently prevent this. To remove these effects a further 'averaging' process is carried out. In order to irradicate this effect the simplest thing to do is to distribute it between 'seasons'.

6.9.6   Predicting the Future

In an intrinsic fashion, all we have so far done is isolate the trend and provide a rationale for the choice of a specific model and thereby establish on average, the seasonal variation. What we can say now, is that given the need to project a trend, we can do that prediction in accordance with our calculated variations and thereby provide a more realistic prediction of what is likely to happen in future periods.

How then is this done? Perhaps a simple example to place what has been said in context will help.

Imagine that you are the risk manager of an hypothetical road transport organisation. You wish to provide your accountants with a quarterly budget for losses for the following year (19-8). Previously you have done this on a rather subjective basis but now you wish to apply some objectivity. You recognise immediately that the problem may be resolved by utilising time series analysis.

You start by obtaining details of relevant, past data. Say, it was as shown in figure 6.20:-

	Quarters			
	1st	**2nd**	**3rd**	**4th**
19-3	65	21	120	34
19-4	71	21	132	36
19-5	83	39	136	42
19-6	89	44	148	59
19-7	107	60	169	74

Figure 6.20: Quarterly Loss Provisions (£000's) 19-3 to 19-7

Already a short-term pattern is evident. Furthermore, in each quarter, the trend is upward. The following figure, which, in essence, is a scattergraph, highlights these features.

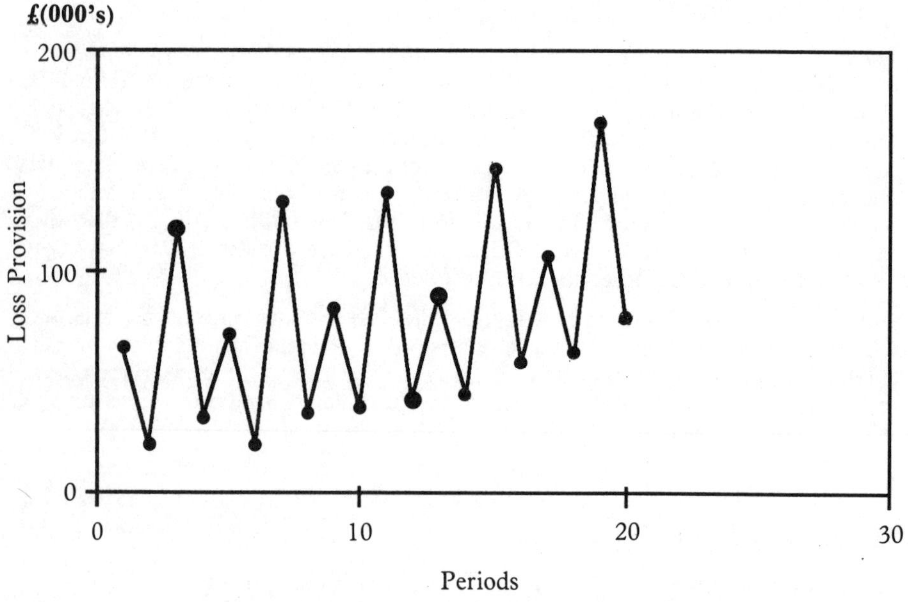

Figure 6.21: Past Losses Graphed over Time

6.9.7 The Line of Best Fit

Clearly, it seems from simple observation that the model is worth developing. Can we gain further support? The reader will recall the debate upon autocorrelation carried out in section **6.5.4.** Here such a lagged correlation should be carried out in order to provide a measure of the degree of association between the various periods. In this instance, lagging the periods by four quarters resulted in a correlation (**r** = +0.99). The Model is worth developing.

Before measuring the trend, the reader must be quite clear in his mind as to the purpose. Usually, there are two reasons behind such measurement; the first of which is projecting the trend (and this can be done by establishing a 'line of best fit'). The second is using the model (provided it is a valid one) to predict forward periods.

Locating the 'line of best fit' is sometimes a matter of judgement, indeed a line may be drawn freehand, and not infrequently it is considered sufficient, though to do this does require care in that the reader must be able to recognise where the cycles and seasonal variations are. This, of course, requires a thorough knowledge of the data under analysis. Usually, however, it is best to resort to an equation. In other words objectivity rather than subjectivity.

The method most generally used is the method of least squares; a method that parallels the method used in regression analysis wherein the line of best fit is mathematically established.

The line again, may be represented by the general equation:-

$$Y = a + bx$$

Where:- y = the dependent variable (the provision))
         a = the value of the trend when y = 0
         b = the change in trend for each change in period
         x = any period value that is selected.
             (usually, consecutive periods are
             represented by numbering them, starting
             from 1 through to n).

As before, the regression equation may be established. Let us say that the relevant constant term and the regression coefficient are such that the resultant trend equation becomes:-

$$y50.895 + 2.534x$$

Given this, we would substitute into the model 'forward' periods, and the equation solved to produce a prediction for **y**, so:-

19-8	Q1:	x = 21	thus y =	104.109
	Q2:	x = 22	thus y =	106.653
	Q3:	x = 23	thus y =	109.177
	Q4:	x = 24	thus y =	111.711

In other words, each quarter of 19-8, shows an increase, on average, of £2,534 over the previous quarter.

Figure 6.22. (overleaf) now graphs the series, and the regression line. It shows that for a given time period there are considerable 'departures' between a predicted value of **Y** and the actual value and hence there is doubt about the validity of our predictions. Indeed further evidence of this doubt would materialise if we were to 'predict' known periods.

6.9.8   Coping with the Departures from the Line of Best Fit

How then can we cope with these departures which we now know to comprise the four components we discussed earlier?

Noticing that some recurring observations are consistently higher than any other; we realise, for example, that the prediction of the third quarter of 19-8 as 109.177

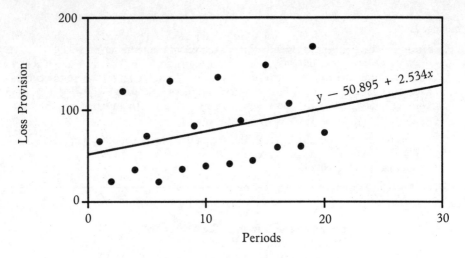

Figure 6.22: Evidence of Departures from the Regression Line

is not realistic. Clearly, we should really add something, the question is how much? Decomposition of the series (the principle of which we discussed earlier) helps resolve the problem and so we must proceed to establish the average seasonal variation.

Procedures exist whereby such variations can be established and any standard spreadsheet facility can cope with required arithmetic. Assuming we were to retain our final seasonal adjustment as:-

	Quarters		
1st	**2nd**	**3rd**	**4th**
9.98	-39.21	61.91	-32.68

then, in the light of this information we are now in a position to revise our predictions to:-

Predicted	Regression	Seasonal	Revised
(Quarter 1)	104.109	+ 9.98	=114.089
(Quarter 2)	106.643	− 39.21	= 67.433
(Quarter 3)	109.177	+69.91	=179.087
(Quarter 4)	111.711	− 32.68	= 79.031

Hence we may say to our accountant, that our predictions for the quarterly budget for 19-8 are:-

Period	£
1st Quarter	114,000
2nd Quarter	67,000
3rd Quarter	179,000
4th Quarter	79,000

Clearly, as new data becomes available, revised predictions may be made and adjustments made within the flexible budgeting system and in the end better management of resources and better ultimate profitability.

Finally, time series analysis makes no provision for controlling losses. In this example, we have an increasing trend and the risk manager's efforts are likely to be exerted upon slowing that trend down and possibly reversing it. This aspect is more a feature of regression analysis which we covered earlier.

6.10   A Concluding Comment on Time Series

In recent years, time series analysis has come to the forefront of the statistical tools used in forecasting future events. Whilst the framework for the examples used has been kept to as simple a level as is reasonably possible, the reader must be sure to realise that time series analysis can be a complex process. The prediction, for example, of oil prices is so fraught with difficulty and so subject to random variables, that the use of time series anlaysis often raises more issues than it resolves. However, that must not be seen in a negative context. Time series at least provides some objectivity to decision making and we find new instances where such procedures are being used including, for example, lawyers who are making increasing use of expert witnesses to testify about the present value of a person's or a firm's future income and the costs incurred from the loss of a job due, for example to tortious circumstances. Clearly, it is advantageous if the risk manager can be a step or two ahead and there can be no doubting that many questions can be answered by the judicious use of time series analysis.

Chapter 7

RISK MANAGEMENT IN INTERNATIONAL CORPORATIONS

7.0   So far we have concentrated on domestic issues and have said nothing about the international dimension of risk management. The techniques which have been introduced in this book, and in other subjects of the Institute's Diploma, can be applied in almost any country. However, we must now turn to the situation where a company transacts business in more than one country. There is no doubt that since the second world war we have seen significant changes in industrial societies. These changes go far beyond anything which we could have imagined and certainly include a considerble growth in international operations.

7.1   GROWTH IN INTERNATIONAL OPERATIONS

This move towards large international concerns has been aided by a number of factors including:

- The ease of transport throughout the world. It is not uncommon for people to cross the Atlantic twice in the same day! It is even technically possible to leave London and arrive in New York before you left! Imagine trying to suggest to someone fifty years ago that all of this global travel would be possible with such ease?

- Communication links have also improved to a point which could hardly have been imagined a decade or two ago. It is now not only possible to pick up a telephone and dial almost anywhere in the world, it is also possible to send the image of a document to the other side of the world in a matter of seconds, and have it printed.

- The substantial developments in certain parts of the world have also fuelled the growth in international business. Areas rich in natural resources, and some not so rich, have emerged as powerful trading nations.

- Finally a hallmark of the world, or at least the western world, is that it has been relatively free from global warfare. This has also assisted the growth in internationlism in industry and precipitated an increasing level of international co-operation.

There are many other factors which could be considered to be as important as those we have listed but the focus of our attention is not so much on the reasons for internationalism, as on the results. The effect can be seen in the annual reports of most large groups. Companies are now trading in fifty, sixty, eighty, one hundred different countries or more. What is the impact of all of this on risk management within these companies?

Each risk manager will have his own opinion as to the effect on himself and his company. The impact will also vary from company to company and indeed from industry type to industry type. What we can do is to itemise what we believe to be the special features of risk management within an international organisation.

7.2 SPECIAL FEATURES OF INTERNATIONAL RISK MANAGEMENT

There are many ways in which the features of international risk management could be listed. We have chosen to group the features under five main headings, but before doing that let us be clear as to what we mean by international risk management.

For the purpose of this section we will say that international risk management is risk management within a genuine international company. The characteristics of such a company would include the following:

- A significant proportion of their income is derived from overseas operations.
- There is a significant capital investment in foreign countries.
- The management of the company has a 'world' perspective in its strategy making.
- There are production or service units in a range of countries.

In one sense the number of countries in which a company operates is important but equally important are the views and attitude of senior management.

One of the most comprehensive studies of risk management in international corporations has been carried out by Dr Norman Baglini. His findings are reported in a book published by the Risk Management Society Publisihing Inc., called Global Risk Management: How U.S. International Corporations Manage Foreign Risks. The book is based on the response of 142 U.S. corporations to a survey questionnaire sent out in 1980. All the responding corporations were member companies of the American Risk and Insurance Management Society.

In an appendix to the book Dr Baglini summarises the problem areas in implementing foreign risk management programmes. This summary included the following:

Rank	Internal communications Including language %	Attitude of local managers %	Currency problems %	Lack of qualified personnel %
1	24	9	0	5
2	21	10	6	7
3	9	10	5	13
4	7	8	6	9
5	9	9	5	14
6	6	9	9	10
7	6	5	9	10
8	6	6	17	10
9	2	15	14	9
10	1	5	13	4
Blank	9	13	17	11

This is only an extract from a much fuller table but it does indicate the kind of problems perceived by those involved in international risk management. We can see that the communication problem looms large for those who have to grapple with it. Notice that currency problems seem much less of a problem. What is a little worrying however, is the large number of blank responses to the currency question, seventeen percent! We can also see from the table that the attitude of local management was ranked one or two by 19% and at the other end of the scale was ranked nine or ten by 20%. There would seem to be a bi-modal distribution at work here, possibly indicating quite sharp differences among responding companies.

Let us now turn to the special features of risk management within these international companies.

7.2.1   The Nature of the Risks

The risks to which a company is exposed are extended if they are operating internationally.

1.   Different perils threaten different parts of the world. Natural risks such as earthquakes, hurricanes and tidal waves are obvious examples of this. The so called political risks also fall in this category with terrorism, confiscation of assets, currency restrictions, nationalisation of assets all being relevant.

2.   Another related point is that the probability of loss will vary from one place to another. Not only is there the possibility that new risks such as earthquake may emerge for the group as a whole, but there may be an earthquake risk in several different countries all with a different likelihood.

3.   A third factor related to the nature of the risk itself is the question of international inter-dependence. We know that even within the one country it may be that one factory or unit can depend on another. This problem can be magnified many times when a number of different countries is involved. This feature of international operations can of course be turned into an advantage where companies make use of their international resources to minimise risk.

7.2.2   Socio-legal Factors

Not only may there be differences in the risks themselves but there may also be differences of a more cultural nature.

1.   Standards vary a great deal throughout the world. This is not in any sense a criticism of different countries but simply an observation. Whether standards are better or worse is a matter of opinion but all who have travelled internationally would agree that standards with regard to risk and its management do differ.

This could be manifested, for example, in different attitudes towards safety or fire prevention or security. Two different countries might attach quite different priorities to the same issue.

2.   Legal systems also differ throughout the world. This is true for civil as well as criminal law and can cause substantial problems if not managed well. We

need only look to the USA to see the substantial differences between their system of compensating the victims of negligence and our own.

7.2.3 Financial Factors

A range of financial implications emerge for the risk manager, when the company for which he works is international.

1. Operating in different currencies is the first real problem. It may not be within the remit of the risk manager to deal with this issue but it is one he should nevertheless recognise. The risk arises due to possible changes in exchange rates. The risk manager may have to settle claims in a foreign country or remit money back to the head office. He may have to pay premiums in local currency, operate a captive which transacts business in a foreign currency etc. There is a range of issues with which he may be involved.

   Dealing with the foreign exchange risk would merit a text on its own but suffice to say at this point that there are a number of steps which can be taken to manage this particular risk. One of the most common is to enter the futures market. If the risk manager knows that a foreign currency is to be transferred to Sterling at the end of a given time period or that he will require to purchase a foreign currency, the risk he runs is that there will be a change in the value of that currency before the period ends.

   The foreign currency could fall in value, in the way that the American dollar did towards the end of 1987 and the start of 1988. In other words he could get more of the foreign currency for a pound Sterling. The problem arises when an amount of the foreign currency has to be changed into Pounds. The reduction in value of the currency means that more of it is required to purchase each pound. The alternative position is that a foreign currency rises in value, less of it is bought for each pound. The difficulty for the risk manager would arise if he had to settle an account or pay a premium etc, in the foreign currency. He will need to spend more in Sterling to buy the same amount of the foreign currency.

   The futures market assists the risk manager by acting a little like the insurance market. The risk manager could enter into a contract to have a certain amount of a foreign currency delivered when it is needed, say in a years time. He agrees the rate of exchange which will be used and is therefore relieved of the risk of it changing to be unfavourable to him. He has transferred the risk to the person with whom he has contracted. The price he pays for this freedom from risk depends upon the rate of exchange when the foreign currency is actually delivered. If the foreign currency has fallen below the rate upon which the contract was based then the measure of the 'premium' he paid for the certainty is the difference between what he contracted to get and what he could have got had he simply waited and ran the risk.

   For example, let us say that the risk manager knows he will require $10,000 in one years time. The current rate of exchange is $1.70 and he can buy dollars to be delivered in one years time at a rate of $1.65. He goes ahead with the bargain. At the end of the year the actual rate of exchange turns out to be $1.75. The comparison is shown below:

Buy at day one:	$10,000 @ $1.70 = £5,882.35
Buy forward:	$10,000 @ $1.65 = £6,060.61
Run the risk:	$10,000 @ $1.75 = £5,714.29

It would have cost £5882.35 to buy $10.000 dollars at the start of the year. This compares to the price he did pay to have £10.000 delivered in one years time, £6060.61. However at day one he did not know which way the dollar exchange rate would move and in order to be relieved of the uncertainty he bought foward. The actual exchange rate turned out to be $1.75 at the end of the year and so, if he had waited until the end of the year he would only have paid £5714.29. In other words he paid £346.32 (£6060.61 − £5714.29) more than he needed to, with the benefit of hindsight. This is a little like saying you paid a premium of £346.32 to have the risk transferred and hence have all the benefits of certainty in your planning and budgeting etc.

2. A second financial consideration relates to exchange control. Exchange control concerns the restrictions which certain countries place on the flow of money out of their country. Britain has no exchange control and so money can be taken out of the country, free of restriction.

    The same is not true for all countries. Almost all countries will exercise some form of control and normally this will revolve around the reasons why money is leaving the country. In very general terms we could say that movements of capital are subject to more severe restrictions than movements of money for the purposes of importing.

    The risk manager should familiarise himself with the nature of any control in the countries where his company operates. He could also want to anticipate reasons why money may have to be moved out of the country eg. the non-availability of replacement machine parts in the country, purchase of specialised machinery etc.

3. A third financial factor is inflation. A loss in the purchasing power of a currency brings with it a consequent increase in most loss costs. In an international setting rates of inflation do vary greatly and the risk manager would want to be aware of the rates in the countries with which he is concerned. He may also want to have some idea of the general trend of inflation rates in those countries. This information is readily available in published form. The IMF International Financial Statistics booklet gives rates of interest, and other financial and economic indicators. A few are shown below and the great variation in rates can be seen quite clearly:

Rates of Inflation
(International Comparison)

	1970	1974	1978	1982	1986
Japan	7.6	23.2	4.2	2.7	0.6
USA	5.9	11.0	7.6	6.2	1.9
UK	6.4	15.9	8.3	8.6	3.5
Argentina	13.6	23.5	175.5	164.8	90.1
Brazil	22.3	27.6	38.7	97.8	145.2
World Avg.	6.1	15.0	9.6	12.6	8.5

(Source: IMF International Financial Statistics)

4.   A final factor is the fact that reinstatement times can vary from country to country. This is linked of course to the problem of inflation. The longer the reinstatement period is and the higher the rate of inflation, then the task of setting realistic sums insured etc, will be made all the more difficult. The problem with reinstatement times could be brought about by a lack of materials or of labour, transport difficulties, protracted negotiations for planning permission following a fire and so on.

7.2.4   Managerial Issues

A further group of special factors relates to managerial or administrative concerns.

1.   General communication problems are obvious areas for administrative difficulties. Apart from any language differences there can be time zones to consider, ambiguities in the use of the same words and phrases. These problems are diminishing as the volume of international business grows, but they still represent a real issue, particularly for the newcomer.

2.   The identification and ultimate control of the risk relies largely on the co-operation of others, particularly those on the shop floor. If the risk manager is not seen to have authority then he may not find the co-operation which is so essential.

   There may indeed be a corporate move towards decentralisation which would make acceptance of a centralised risk management function very difficult. It is important that the risk manager is not seen as a distant 'head office' character. He must strive to create a good working relationship with overseas contacts. This takes time and patience but the reward can be the kind of partnership between the risk manager and personnel which is essential to the effective management of risk in the company as a whole.

7.2.5   Political Risks

Political risk exposure is one of the distinguishing features of companies which are international. The direct physical loss and the possibly more worrying 'unseen' risks have been a feature of international activity for many years. The level of political risk has been steadily increasing over recent years and there are now specialist consultancies which offer advice on managing the political risk. For our purposes we will look at this under two headings.

1.   Firstly there is the direct physical loss of assets as in the case of war or other acts of terrorism. In addition companies also have to contend with the actions of foreign governments in the expropriation or confiscation of assets. The respondents to the Baglini survey reported expropriation losses in Iran, Nicaragua, Portugal, El Salvador, Peru, Jamaica, Lebanon, Algeria and Madagascar, among others.

2.   The second problem is the attack on personnel. Kidnap and ransom is no longer only the stuff of fiction. In 1980, fifty seven of the corporations which responded to the Baglini survey, reported having had an executive kidnapped.

3.   The third point to make is that foreign governments can pose a threat without having to go the length of confiscating assets. Import or export

licenses can be withdrawn, sudden and unforseen restrictions can be placed on manufacturing activities, things can just be made 'difficult'.

7.3   CONCLUSION

The whole area of international risk management is one which, like many other topics in risk management, could constitute a book on its own. What we have done here is to raise the fundamental points which make international risk management different from a pure domestic situation. It is not indended to be a comprehensive study of international programmes.

Chapter 8

DISASTER AND CONTINGENCY PLANNING

Contents

8.1   Introduction

It seems apposite to start this chapter with an attempt at defining Contingency Planning. Needless to say this is a somewhat difficult task and is akin to responding to the question concerning the length of a piece of string. Frequently synonyms to Contingency Planning are often found yet there are subtle differences between these and about when the reader should be aware. Among them are such terms as Disaster Planning, Emergency Planning and Crisis Management. Perhaps we could try to draw a distinction between them; a distinction that to some might be fine but which the following diagram might now place in context:—

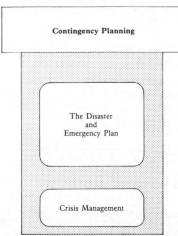

Fig 8.1 — Contingency Planning and its Constituent Elements

Take Disaster and Emergency Planning. This is really the first in a line of defence; it is this plan that the competent risk manager puts in place in order to prevent the occurence of some potentially disasterous event with the Emergency Plan element of that plan being an 'interim' measure until emergency services are in place. On the other hand, Crisis Management is post event. In other words, the disaster takes place, the disaster and emergency plan comes into effect with Crisis Management as a follow-up. The point is that these features seem complementary; indeed they are for they are component parts of contingency planning; the disaster and emergency plan is there to prevent and crisis management to cure... and we all know that prevention is better than cure!

8.2   The Aim of Contingency Planning

Let us put Contingency Planning into context. For a moment consider the risks implicit in the computing operations of a major, international Organisation. There are environmental risks and risks to the system itself; there are the traditional external risks (for example overload damage to software, defective design and data media corruption). There are the risks of fraud and those of contravention of the data processing legislation; there are risks inherent in its management and the consequences of the loss of key personnel. There are the risks of surge, failure and reduction of the power supply and so on. Within the framework of this example, we have only considered one aspect of that hypothetical organisation's operation yet it is clearly a minefield of possibilities, the list can be almost endless.

Let us now take the example a stage further. As risk manager to that Company, you are awakened early one Sunday morning to be told that there has been a major explosion in your Company's warehouse and that the resultant fire was spreading. By the time you reach the scene you find that the Company's entire data processing centre with all relevant accounting records has been destroyed. Perhaps the loss of the buildings — even although it cost millions of pounds could be survived but what of the computing records? Loss of these could be sufficient to put you out of business.

"That's OK",

We hear you say,

"I have back-up materials, programs and documents".

Albeit you consider yourself safe, the hard truth of the matter is that in a ten-year period, there were in excess of 350 major data processing disasters, many of which put the relevant firms out of business. Another interesting piece of information (and here we are considering *only one* hazard) in excess of 40% of those Companies which suffer a disasterous fire loss never trade again. There is substantial evidence that points to Organisations becoming so dependent upon their key activities (such as data processing) that, given a disaster does occur there remains an uncertainty as to their survival... yet again, prevention is better than cure and a contingency plan is one step forward in reducing that uncertainty.

8.3   Some 'Authoritative' Views

It is all very well to consider the matter via an hypothetical business example, but what of the more macro perspective of Government? What is their view? Their demands for contingency planning are evidenced through a variety of Government Bodies, Agencies and relevant reports. For example, directly through The Offshore Installation Regulations (Emergency Procedures), and indirectly, through The Health and Safety at Work Act 1974. Additionally, there are the rules and procedures laid down by The Health and Safety Executive. What, then, of the "independents"? Among these are to be found the Joint Chemical Industries Association/Insurers Standing Committee and its reports on risk assessment. Yet are these but lip service? In other arenas, Government, for example is clearly less helpful. Consider, for a moment the financial implications of a disaster. Clearly it requires considerable resources to recover from a disaster yet in such planning Government seems reticent to allow the creation of contingency reserves as allowable against tax.

Why then bother with the process? The reasoning is clear. Businesses need to make profits if they are to survive. Businesses today cannot afford to be without supplies (nor their suppliers) for lengthy times and competitors are always waiting in the wings to snap up any opportunity that may arise. Clearly contingency planning is a desirable commodity to help prevent such issues arising and as a tool, contingency planning is one that most organisations should not fail to have — no matter their size. Paradoxically, and all too often, a potential loss situation is considered as far too remote or insignificant a possibility as to be worth paying attention to. Dare we say it again... prevention is better than cure!

As a process, contingency planning ensures that an Organisation is on the correct path to resume its critical business operations and within an acceptable time frame after a disaster has occurred. To do this effectively allows the Organisation to maintain its "competitive edge". In short, the aim of contingency planning is to minimise the effect of the unwanted occurrence no matter how remote.

Clearly, small interruptions to the flow of business are a norm for most Organisations but there must be some cut-off point beyond which a normally acceptable position turns into one which is not; in other words the financial consequences now attain "disasterous" proportions. Of course, the fact that one Organisation, in a set of specific circumstances, has a disaster does not necessarily mean that a second, when faced with mirror image circumstances, considers that it has one. "Disasters" then are relative. There is no common thread. Conceptually and in Organisational terms, it is 'personal'. Bearing in mind such caveats, then it might be useful to try and distinguish between what might constitute a major risk and that which might fall into the category of a "disaster". Perhaps the distinction should be placed within a normal/catastrophic continueum. Think, for a moment of the environment in which you, the reader, work. Imagine a fire of a "normal" magnitude. It might cause little harm; perhaps little by way of serious injury or extensive damage in the circumstances such an occurrence is unlikely to fall within the definition of a disaster. Take the matter a stage further and have a loss where there is some harm, it is only marginal and does not significantly affect normal operating procedures. In such a scenario, albeit considered as adverse, there remains doubt as to whether the consequences attain disaster proportions. If, however, the fire was major and catastrophic in its nature and did cause considerable injury and extensive damage and was of such proportions that it required the use of outside resources to handle it effectively, then it is highly likely that it would be considered a 'disaster'. Whilst we have used fire as an example the parallel could equally be drawn using say toxic materials or hazardous chemicals. Indeed, any dangerous situation could be considered as being disasterous but it can only be considered as such within the context of your business.

Implicit in what has been said is that contingency planning is solely concerned with the macro-economic aspects of the firm. That is not so, for it is a tool that equally can be used in the operating unit within an Organisation. That this is so raises an issue of "acceptability" for, as we have seen, what is a "disaster" to one Organisation might not affect the Organisation as a whole yet when considered within the context of the small part of that Organisation would provide serious disruption. Contingency Planning is just as relevant here. The impact of a disaster on a single profit centre within a corporate structure should not be underestimated; neither should the "knock-on" effect for this could result in substantial financial repercussions to the Company as a whole. Anything that threatens an Organisation's financial stability must be prevented and Contingency Planning is one process towards obtaining that goal.

On a wider issue, public pressure, legislation provisions, and social and cultural change all demand that businesses have a greater awareness of the consequences of a possible disaster; a disaster which may not only affect the business but also affect the environment within which others live. Businesses must try to — but might not — prevent these from occurring. Contingency Planning might help.

8.4   Is Contingency Planning Risk Management?

It seems to us that contingency planning somewhat reflects the basics of risk management but it is not our intention to cover the whole of that topic again! Essentially, are we not talking of the identification, the analysis of and the control of, risk? Does not the Risk Management procedure set itself out to prepare a plan that will implement a preventative course of action? In this case the occurrence is special; it is of disaster proportions. Indeed the whole of the risk management process could be described as contingency planning, which latter process has, as we have seen, two component parts:—

1. The Disaster and Emergency Plan, concerned with loss prevention and control.

and 2. The Crisis Management Plan, concerned with reducing the risk should the disaster occur.

What is clear is the need to distinguish between those disruptions to a business which are minor or short term and which arguably fall into the routine, day-to-day nature of risk management. On the other hand, there are those risks which are major and cause substantial disruption and which tend to have a significant impact upon a business. It is not sufficient simply to discuss these risks on the assumption that the chance of their occurrence is very low for the result of a failure to handle them properly could lead to an unacceptable interruption — indeed cessation of — business. It is to these latter risks that Contingency Planning is particularly relevant and which procedurally sets out to minimise the effect of their impact upon an Organisation.

Prevention is better than cure no matter how remote the likelihood!

8.5   Pinning The Responsibility for Contingency Planning

We are considering in this chapter, those risks the consequences of which are of disasterous proportions. Because of this, it is essential that the management of any serious interruption is pinned to a key executive. We shall, for the sake of convenience, title this person the "Disaster Executive". So, responsibilities start with the Disaster Executive, but how and who do you select?

Certainly, the Disaster Executive will have a number of attributes among them:—

1. Familiarity with the facilities of the Organisation and its hazards.
2. Knowledge of the protective systems that are in place (for example, the sprinkler and the burglar alarm systems).
3. Familiarity with salvage and rescue facilities.
4. An understanding of fire sciences; not only in terms of ordering and control, but also in terms of combining forces with other public departments.

Clearly, it is for the Organisation to select whom it consideres to be the best person. Whoever is chosen, that person must be a leader and have his decisions respected despite the fact that they may rub against the grain of people who, in normal circumstances, may be the Disaster Executive's superiors.

Whilst some may consider the Chief Executive of their Organisation as the relevant person to take over the role, it need not necessarily be so. Indeed we would argue that it should be someone else, for Chief Executives are too close to 'normal' operations and too remote from the realities of a catastrophe scenario. Indeed they might lack the essential attributes suggested above.

Additionally, it must be remembered that when appointed, and when acting in a disaster situation that the Disaster Executive is effectively acting on behalf of the Chief Executive and the Organisation's policy statement should clearly reflect that that is the case. Whoever the Disaster Executive is, that person must assume the role of Chief Executive for among the latter's responsibilities is the prevention of collapse and it is the Chief Executive who is accountable should the Organisation's survival be in doubt. The Chief Executive and top management must be supportive, for the Disaster Executive's decisions may well counter the aims of normal operations. Decisions may seem to counter reality but it must be made clear that what the Disaster Executive says, goes! Top management must want an Organisation that can act immediately in the event of a disaster taking place and for this reason authority and responsibility must be delegated effectively should that disaster occur.

8.6   The Planning Team

In setting up a Contingency Plan, there is a need for the Disaster Executive to form a planning team. Its purpose is clear; it is to identify the risks, prepare the plan. Whoever that team is, it needs to act quickly so as to "batten down the hatches" should the disaster occur. It is important to identify key personnel within the Organisation who will assist in the planning of the recovery operation and building the detailed infrastructure essential to its effective operation. Furthermore, there should be a succession list so that in the event of a disaster, there are staff available to take over key operations and clear guidelines must be given to those who are to take over from them.

In conclusion, there must be overall control if contingency planning is to be effective. Leaving it to individual departments may mean an ineffective return to normality because of competing interests. Planning is in the interest of the "whole" not the "parts". Commitment must be absolute and adequate provision must be made for deputies so that in the absence of assigned staff, their responsibilities can continue.

8.7 Formulating A Contingency Plan

So far we have considered the framework within which Contingency Planning should be set but what about its formation? How do we put such a plan together?

8.7.1 Identification

As a first step it is essential for the planning team, in their endeavours, to identify those areas of the business where there is the likelihood, no matter how remote, of serious interruption to the business.

Thus, for example, a thorough inventory of the Company's assets and an assessment of the consequences of a possible catastrophe is only one part of the process. If we were to consider a possible inventory of such property then a catastrophic fire might result in:—

1. Loss of Profits
2. Loss of Market
3. Loss of Goodwill
4. Increased Costs
5. Exposure to potential take-over
6. Possible winding-up

Such losses might be no different for those Organisations who suffer from a significant breakdown in their data processing services or those who suffer the after effects of a large explosion. Whatever the case, it is clear that senior management must consider the impact of such possible major disasters.

We have already made mention of the possible knock-on effects to a business and for this reason it is essential to identify, in that area, the potential risks. Clearly the process is complex but if the disaster team centres upon the traditional attributes of the risk management process wherein are established such matters as loss frequencies and severities, the needs for loss prevention measures and finally the procedures essential for a disaster plan, then the team is well on the way to fulfilling its responsibilities. In effect what is required of the disaster team is the application of the traditional techniques of risk management.

For example, consider flow charting. The disaster team would be will advised to chart the entire organisational process. It should account for its suppliers and its customers; for its machines, its operators, its labour and its key personnel; it should account for sales supporting operations such as packaging and distribution. Hazard analysis and operability studies are additional techniques that will assist the team to establish where it is likely that 'something could go wrong'. We have already made mention of the need not to ignore those instances where the chance of loss is so small that it may be considered negligible. It's rather like the nuclear explosion; the chance may be low but when it happens? The business parallel is no less dramatic. The impact could be considerable and that aspect must never be lost.

The disaster team must be objective in its approach and recognise the possibly diverse nature of the Organisation of which it forms a part. There are many industrial Organisations, which have very large operations, which if struck by a disaster, would suffer significantly. However, the disaster team's risk survey must not discount matters simply on the basis of size.

Additionally, it would be to any disaster team's advantage in this identification process to have available relevant survey reports, site plans, process flow charts and so on.

There is also the need to establish where there is protection and to assess the potential effect on satellite units. Clearly, there is no substitute for being systematic. To be so produces the relative success stories in the contingency planning process.

8.7.2   Evaluation

Having successfully established where the risks are, the next logical stage is their evaluation. This is important, for in addition to establishing what risks actually affect the business one must also consider the likelihood of them arising.

The disaster team must consider many features, for example there will be timescale implications in that recovery will be seriously delayed in the face of long replacement lead times. How can this be handled? Matters of stand-by equipment should be considered. Should it be remote? What of production capability? Can satellites cope? Can off-site storage cope? Are new production techniques better? Are they available? Are there any special production priorities? What will be the effect on sales? Any seasonal demands? Further questions arise which centre upon the financial implications. What for example, are the additional costs — fixed and variable? Are there any contractual penalty clauses that will have to be honoured? What about key personnel? redundancies? alternative employment? The list is almost endless but the astute team will not rest in its endeavours to consider all aspects in evaluating the scale of the problem.

The end result of this evaluative process is to establish the levels of exposure and then to agree on the method to be used in calculating these. It is the latter aspect that is perhaps the most difficult element in the contingency planning process and it is impossible in a general text such as this to come up with any definitive model. The method is clearly a function of the Organisation and the nature of the information system it posesses. Certainly, it is essential to quantify the exposure and in that context, the accounting data is perhaps a crucial source.

The evaluative process is important as it will help rank matters in terms of their risk profiles. This helps the disaster team to prioritise those areas where there is a relatively high disaster exposure; an area which the disaster team will have to target.

Clearly, minimisation of the interruption hazard comes to mind and proper evaluation will give the disaster team the 'room' to centre upon prevention in key areas.

Once these risks have been identified and their consequences evaluated then the disaster team can turn to controlling — even eliminating some of the relevant risks by appropriate risk control methods and to formulating their Disaster and Emergency Plan.

8.8   The Disaster and Emergency Plan

It is arguably the case that disasters fall into two major categories, there are those that are of a 'natural' form and those that are, what we might call, 'man-made'. The distinction is clear; the former comprises such events as flood, earthquake, storm and tempest as evidenced in the UK in the latter end of 1987 and the early part of 1988. The latter include the likes of explosion, and pollution; even political risk may be considered as 'man-made'. Whatever the cause, the common denominator in preparation of the plan is the assumption that the consequences are substantial and the event has occurred. The first aspect of contingency planning is the preparation of the disaster and emergency plan. This plan has an almost single goal namely dealing with the consequential aspects of the event occurring rather than dealing with the cause. When the disaster occurs it is too late to stop it! For example, the plan sets out in a pre-emptive fashion, to deal with the consequences of say, a major air collision over the City of London or the consequences of an underground disaster such as occurred at King's Cross Underground Station. Such a plan does not centre upon the reasons as to why the event occurred. The plan comes into effect as soon as the event occurs and continues to remain in place until the emergency services take over.

8.8.1   Formulating The Disaster and Emergency Plan

Clearly, this concept of planning is concerned with raising the "confidence level" in an organisation's ability to recover effectively and clearly, this confidence is a function of the quality of that plan. In our earlier discussions, we saw how there must be committment by management and how it must be controlled by a 'senior person'; but what are the elements of the plan? In essence there is no standard model, but *figure 8.2* following outlines the framework and it gives general pointers towards what should be considered in its contents:–

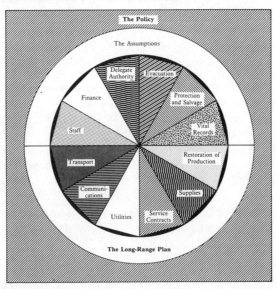

Fig 8.2 — The Constituent Elements of a Disaster and Emergency Plan

Let us now consider each element in isolation.

(1) The Policy
The importance of this element must not be underestimated; it must lay down the basic assumptions of the plan — in other words it identifies the bases which the Organisation had decided to follow in order to provide interim measures and ultimately recovery from the identified, potential disaster. It is analogous to a company's policy statement.

(2) The Long-Range Plan.
It is essential that the disaster team has a competent understanding of its company's organisational structure and its objectives. Not only is there a need to know what its structure and its objectives are *before* a potential disaster; there is also the need to know what they will be should the potential disaster take place. This latter aspect is particularly important given the acquisitive management styles of the late 80's. Such issues must be decided at the planning stage for failure to understand where it is that the company is going could in itself have disasterous implications.

(3) Delegating Authority
We have already seen how there must exist clear delegation of authority. It is worth re-emphasising that time is of the essence in such situations and that there must be an "Organisation-Wide" respect for this essential element. If there is no respect for such authority then the plan, when put into effect, will surely fail?

(4) Evacuation
This seems too obvious to be worth stating yet an ineffective evacuation plan can cause more harm than good. Consideration must be given to the availablity of hospital and medical facilities, first aid facilities — even blood donors! Like the good scout, be prepared.

(5) Protection and Salvage
Remember, the pre-emptive role of the Plan; its role, is somewhat forward looking in that the planning process should initiate current preventative techniques in order to minimise the likelihood of the disaster arising. However, the disaster team must also have a plan which considers those preventative aspects which will be put in place so as to stop further damage occurring. Additionally, the plan must deal competently with the salvage aspects of a disaster. Many a loss situation is significantly reduced because there is in hand a sound plan for dealing with salvage when the disaster occurs.

(6) Vital Records
Most organisations have records that are key to their operation. We have already discussed in this chapter the possible consequences of significant damage to a computer centre. Duplication is obvious; off-site storage is obvious, dealing with such specialist firms who hire complete computing operations is obvious, yet there are clear deficiences in them all. These must be considered too. Data and information recovery must be quick and must be formulated in such a fashion that they do not leave the user departments in isolation. Indeed this latter aspect is very important; only too often are disaster recovery plans in this arena deficient; they take no account of the

user — frequently there are inadequate procedures, plans and resources. There are, of course other vital records and the dangers are really no different. For example, there will be technical data such as engineering specifications; there will be moulds, patterns, drawings, plans and sketches, contracts, leases, personnel records and minutes of board meetings. All must be considered.

(7) Restoration of Production.

Again, the sooner production is recovered the better. Pre-disaster suggestions on how best to handle this aspect might be to separate operating units and if this is a pre-determined initiative then it should be done now rather than later. Whatever is decided, the route to restoration must be clear; the team must carefully think through the process so that when the disaster occurs they know which way to turn.

(8) Supplies.

Not only does the disaster team need to know what it is that will be needed in the event of a disaster, they will need to know from where to obtain the supplies. Who are they? What is the supply lead time? How best can supplies be secured? Where possible, risk minimisation techniques should take place so that when the emergency arises, alternatives are reasonably in place.

(9) Service Contacts.

Organisations cannot operate without others. They all need their suppliers, their customers, their professionals (for example, lawyers, accountants and brokers). Alienate yourselves from them during normal operations and you will have difficulties when the disaster occurs. These people must be taken with you in a co-operative fashion, from day 1. Who to turn to, on what matter and in what eventuality must clearly be established prior to the event.

(10) Provision of Utilities

In a disaster situation, recovery could be relatively quick except where there is a more 'permanent' loss of essential fuels. Back-up power, water and gas facilities, where appropriate, must be in position. Within that context it is essential to know what are the critical services that will be required and to have these on hand now.

(11) Communications.

There is the need to consider the provision of 'incident" facilities. For example a control centre is essential. Clearly in a major disaster, communications must be maintained and such a centre would act as a focus. It should be well resourced including perhaps radio and celnet phone facilities. PA systems, specialist messenger service must all be considered if recovery is to be quick. It must be decided prior to the event how you contact people, what people need to be contacted and what of the various facilities should be used.

(12) Transport.

The availability of required vehicles, as well as alternative transport systems, should be well documented. Know what you will need and where it is you will find it. Have such facilities ready.

(13) Staff.

A disaster and emergency plan should consider the staffing 'problem'. If the disaster occurs, who will work where? Where do they live? How can they be contacted? Special skill might be needed. What are the special skills available? What special skills will be needed? What is the extent of skill transfer? Who will take over the duties of those specially required?

In other words, an inventory of staff, their skills, their transferability is essential, not after the disaster but before it!

(14) Finance.

Perhaps the most important asset to most Organisations is their workforce. It is important that they are paid. For this reason be sure to lay on early plans for their continuing payment. Essential too, are the funding arrangements that will be necessary to help your Organisation to recover. Additional loan facilities; letters of credit and so on may be needed. The planning process, if competently handled, will place matters within a financial framework. If recovery needs a £2m line of credit then be well advised to set up these arrangements; don't leave it until the event occurs. Not least, within the context of the financial element of the plan, is the need to address the insurance arrangements!

Clearly, the disaster and emergency plan, once completed, is there to reduce the uncertainty associated with recovery from say, the effects of a significant explosion. The plan certainly concerns itself with establishing what are the hazards and one of its roles is that of risk containment. We have seen how, in the planning process, eventualities were considered, preventative measures put in place and plans laid down on a "what-if" basis. But what happens when the explosion strikes? It is here that we find its secondary role; a role that comes into effect the minute the disaster takes place. When the planning measures operate on a "when it has occurred" basis, then it must deal with such matters as the:–

    1. Immediate management of internal resources.
    2. Employment of essential external resources.
and the 3. Implementation of damage containment initiatives.

In effect, the plan is now short-term; its sets out the action required between the occurrence of the disaster and the arrival of the emergency service. Much of what the team will require to do will have been thought through in the disaster planning stage and 'for this reason it is essential that these plans are well documented.

8.9　The Crisis Management Plan

What then of the crisis management plan — or, as it is sometimes known, the recovery plan? In this instance, the event has taken place and hence this plan is post disaster, but starting with it.

As its remit is to return the business to an effective operation then as assessment of the effect of the disaster is required. Clearly, the time frame is somewhat longer than that of the disaster and emergency plan. Arguably, then, among this plan's requirements will be a need to centre upon those aspects of the business which are profitable rather than simply providing a contribution to costs. The organisation of such a plan is not unlike that of the disaster and emergency plan and equally requires good risk identification techniques; techniques that will help assess the resource requirements that will ensure that the business returns to normality as quickly as possible.

"Normality", of course implies something of the nature of indemnity, namely placing the organisation in the same position as it was prior to the loss. Nothing could be further from the truth; it is perfectly reasonable for recovery to take account of potential changes in an Organisation's structure; for potential changes in its production methods, indeed any other changes that were anticipated, or those that arise as a consequence of, the disaster. For example, a manufacturer of rubber compounds may be developing a new synthetic alternative. There is no need for the 'old' process to be rebuilt following a disaster, neither is it essential that it produces at the same site. By implication, then, a contingency plan should result in such questions as:—

1. Do we manufacture elsewhere?
2. Do we change the product design?
3. Do we use new machinery?
4. Do we manufacture a product that previously we bought?
5. Do we rebuild?
6. Do we re-design processes?

being asked and then answered so that when the disaster occurs, plans can be put into effect.

It is now that plans, drawings and other essential records are needed so as to reduce the risks of further loss; it is now that alternative premises may be needed; that plant requires to be replaced; that support from identified others is required; that stock management comes to the fore. Procedures are set in motion to assess the physical extent of the disaster and the salvage needs. It is now that central co-ordination is essential; no recovery plan should be done in isolation of the constituent sections of an Organisation — no matter how redundant the section may be felt to be.

8.10   Personnel Training

The fact that businesses are considering the possibility of a disaster, are assessing risks, are putting preventative measures in place and formulating an appropriate plan is a major step forward in 'legitimising the contingency planning process in personnel's eyes. This provides for a senario in which staff realise that there is a real need for training for a disaster and thus it is arguable that the plan will become more effective. Creation of an environment of increasing awareness of the consequences of such an unwanted event might lessen the liklihood of it arising.

Additionally, the plan, should set out to educate management. It will provide a learning mechanism for them too. In other words it must be used to prevent a recurrence and give pointers to the preventative techniques that ought to be applied.

The disaster team must ensure that all personnel are adequately trained to cope. Clearly, training schedules must be determined. The programme must be custom made to the Organisation; it must be imaginative and interesting and designed to bring confidence of recovery when the disaster occurs. All staff must understand, not only how, but why. They must be confident in the use of protective equipment and have confidence in reacting to hazards and in the handling of materials.

Training is a most important catalyst to a successful contingency plan. All personnel must be made aware of the potential implications of their actions during an emergency. Relevant personnel must know what it is they are supposed to do (and, importantly, what it is they are not to do). Communications are essential not only between relevant personnel but by them. Personal coping mechanisms must be maximised.

8.11   Maintaining the Corporate Image

Earlier, mention was made of The Health and Safety Executive. Their documentation suggests some of the features outlined in our discussions on the constituent parts of a model plan. Their suggestions also include the need for good communications with, for example fire, salvage, police and other emergency services; with utility providers the meteoroligical officers and others, among them, nearby firms, subcontractor, suppliers, architects, quantity surveyors and so on. Of these we have already made brief mention.

It is clear that communications must be good; and planning for them is necessary and within this framework the maintenance of a good public image is paramount. It must be carefully handled. There should be a central focus for all information flowing from the Company both at an emergency and crisis management stages. Statements must be authoritative; there must be adequate handling of the aggressive media representative. Matters should be channelled through competent persons (not necessarily a Company employee either); there are so many instances where the image of a company has been unnecessarily tarnished by an incompetent handling of its image and with the inevitable end result being recovery delays.

8.12   Testing

Another important aspect of a contingency plan, yet probably one that has been least frequently put in place, is to test it. We are not so naive as to suggest that one should create an actual disaster to test the plan but what major city has 'closed-down' on the assumption that two-jumbo jets have collided over the city centre? What Industrial Organisation has voluntarily 'shut-down' its entire production system on the assumption that there has been a major explosion? What member of the services industry has 'switched off' its computer system on the assumption that there has been a major corruption of software? Who has really tested their plan? We would suggest few, yet in some ways it is essential that that is done (or is simulated) otherwise there remains the uncertainty as to whether or not the plan will work!

8.13   A Concluding Comment

What is clear is that any contingeny plan must be based upon sound loss prevention and control, techniques. Careful deliberation is required in creating the plan and once established the plan should be well documented and disseminated to all employees. Roles must be clear; the what and how must be clearly established before the disaster occurs. There must be continuing feed back so that plans can be updated; there must be a well-managed review process so that loopholes can be investigated and gaps in the fence filled. In the end, a properly designed and well thought out plan will be a major step forward in dealing with that unexpected and unwanted event, which if it takes place will have a significant effect upon the Organisation; in other words the disaster.

Thus we have it, contingency planning in a nutshell; a subject that is as broad as it is long, a procedure that is no recipe for success but is a long way towards it. Certainly, it is a commodity that should be well sought after. It is a tool that is as essential as risk management itself. Every day we hear of some company that has been destroyed perhaps it will be yours next! To pre-plan for a disaster seems common sense yet how many Organisations have developed such a plan? Clearly it is better to be prepared than not and we all know the extent of the 'good' decisions that are made under conditions of stress! There is nothing new in contingency planning; indeed, in many instances all it needs is the provision of logical thought to knowledge that for many organisations already exists. As a plan it ought to exist yet it is one that you hope not to use; there is nothing hypothetical about it; it is a valuable management tool whose benefits must not be discounted.

Chapter 9

CASE STUDIES

9.0   The bulk of this text has been concerned with the broader more corporate aspects of risk management. We have looked at the role of the risk manager and the structure and location of the risk management department itself. We then moved on to consider the whole area of decision making and the analysis of decisions. This was followed by a brief examination of the role of forecasting in business. International risk management and disaster planning were the final topics covered.

However, the topics dealt with in this text are not all that there is to know about risk management. The other eight subjects of the Institute's Diploma syllabus must be combined with this final subject before the full picture can be appreciated. This *integration* of different pieces of information is all important in building up a comprehensive knowledge in risk management. All the various subject areas have a part to play but they must be integrated in such a way as to make them useful in a practical and applied manner.

Integrating diverse areas of study is not an easy matter. We are used to learning in compartments, where the knowledge gained in one compartment does not have to be transferred to another. This difficulty has to be overcome if we are to practise risk management effectively. Knowledge of safety and occupational health must be combined with what we know of the law in order to ensure that a safe system of work is being operated. Changes in the system must be considered from the financial point of view as well as from any intrinsic merit in reducing losses. The full impact of potential losses must be analysed and comparisons made with the cost of insurance protection. Alternative risk financing mechanisms have to be examined and evaluated. Physical measures for the control of risk must be explored and the costs calculated in accordance with normal accounting procedures. The list could go on and on. All the different strands of knowledge have their part to play and, while we have studied them in individual subjects, we must not look on them as mutually exclusive.

In this final chapter we have produced a number of small case studies which attempt to show the practical application of some of the principles and techniques examined during the course of study for the Diploma. Even those who are reading this text as non-students may find the studies of interest and some value.

9.1   RAPID DELIVERIES PLC.

Rapid Deliveries has been in business for some time and specialises in the rapid delivery of parcels within city centres. Its operations are concentrated in London, Leeds and Glasgow, they employ the same number of people at each depot and operate the same number of vehicles from each. The fleet is made up of small vans and estate cars, it is a relatively new fleet as vehicles are replaced when three years old.

The company has been quite happy to take its share of the delivery market but in recent years an increasing number of competing firms have arrived on the scene offering rates below what Rapid considers economic. As a result they have been forced to trim costs, at one end, and think of new areas of business, at the other. One potential source of new business is the delivery of letters along with the parcels. They are well geared up to handle letters and parcels. A slight modification in the terms of employment of its workforce would be required but no major difficulty is foreseen. They feel that a good service could be offered to those who already use Rapid for parcel delivery. They would confine the service to major city centres. The marketing manager has been examining the feasibility of this plan for some time and has written to all managers asking for their input. So far their has been a response from the finance manager, the fleet manager and the company secretary. The deadline by which a response is to be made is approaching.

On the question of expenses, the company has been examining ways to keep costs as low as possible and a number of stringent steps have been taken already. The finance director is anxious that every manager does all that he can to explore possible cost savings in his own area. The major cost that you have is that of accidental damage claims on the motor fleet. You cancelled the insurance cover on this some years ago and have been carrying the risk ever since, the third party risk is still insured.

You have the feeling that the absence of insurance has acted as a disincentive to the fleet manager. His accidental damage claims are currently paid out of current revenue and not debited to his operation. He has argued that he is as careful as he always has been but that the increasing use of agency drivers has not helped. Agency drivers are necessary at certain times of the year in order to cope with excessive demand. The fleet manager keeps a record of all accidental damage claims, whether they involved an agency driver or not and the month in which the accident occurred. You have asked for a copy of his record for the last full year. It is attached.

RAPID DELIVERY — ACCIDENT BOOK

COST	DRIVER	LOCATION	MONTH
100	own	London	April
1650	agency	Glasgow	December
200	agency	Leeds	June
375	own	London	August
4000	agency	Glasgow	January
350	agency	Leeds	September
575	agency	London	August
264	own	London	April
300	own	London	June
145	own	Leeds	April
1000	agency	Glasgow	April
750	agency	Leeds	July
240	own	London	October
220	own	London	September
3750	agency	Glasgow	February
865	agency	Leeds	March
145	own	Leeds	May
120	own	London	June
1700	agency	Glasgow	October

2300	agency	Glasgow	February
350	own	Leeds	July
432	own	Leeds	October
1780	agency	Glasgow	April
1500	agency	Glasgow	May
280	own	Leeds	May
2450	agency	Leeds	January
200	own	Leeds	August
190	agency	Glasgow	November
390	own	Leeds	September
2700	agency	Leeds	June
464	own	London	October
160	own	London	July
122	own	Leeds	July
2500	own	Glasgow	January
2850	agency	London	December
3000	agency	London	November
1000	own	Glasgow	November
140	own	London	September
3600	agency	Glasgow	December
110	own	London	March
125	own	Leeds	August
500	own	Leeds	October
1700	own	Glasgow	February
150	own	Leeds	June

9.1.1   Here we have three different strands all running at the same time. There is the potential launch of a new product in the form of letter deliveries, the analysis of the loss experience of the fleet for accidental damage claims and the examination of possible alternative risk financing mechanism.

We can see, in this relatively simple example, a number of different areas of expertise being required.

1. The new product launch.

Aspects of law and business economics creep into this section of the study. A general knowledge of the business environment would be necessary so that any comments from the risk point of view could be made without appearing to be commercially unaware.

2. Loss Analysis

To address this section of the study a person would need to have some knowledge of statistical risk analysis. In addition it is necessary to be able to report the results of the analysis in a manner which others will understand. As a result, the skill of report writing is also called upon.

3. Funding of losses

The many techniques for the financing of risk are what is being asked for in this section of the study. In addition there may well be the need for behavioural input. There is the feeling that the fleet manager is not as careful as he has been, possibly because the insurance cover has been cancelled and he sees no direct link between claims and costs.

We cannot provide full worked solutions to all the studies in this chapter, this would involve the production of a book many times the size of the current volume. However, as an illustration of what is involved let us look at the kind of report which could be made on the second problem, that of the loss experience.

RAPID DELIVERIES PLC

Details have been gathered on 44 accidents over the past year. There is information on the eventual settlement cost, the month in which the accident took place, the depot the vehicle operated from and whether or not the driver was employed by Rapid or was an agency employee. The information is restricted to accidental damage and hence no data is available for claims involving injury to any person or damage to property other than the vehicle.

The average cost of damage is £1078 with claims ranging from £100 to £4000. The bulk of the claims were in the lower range of money, 61% of all claims were for amounts less than £1000 and 80% were for amounts less than £2000. This follows the pattern which one would expect from incidents of this type. The data available does however allow us to look a little more closely at the origin of some of the claims.

Depots

The vehicles operated from three depots. The Leeds depot accounted for 40% of all claims with the other two depots sharing the remainder equally. The real number of claims is however not as important as the eventual cost of the incidents. While Glasgow may only have produced 30% of the claims it did account for 60% of the total cost. Leeds on the other hand only produced 21% of the total claims figure. Fig (1) shows the division of claims costs over the three depots.

CLAIMS COSTS

SPLIT BETWEEN DEPOTS

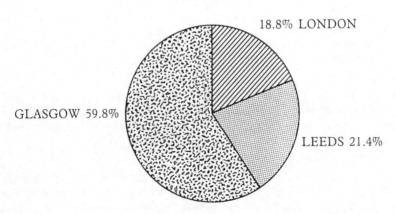

Fig 1

Drivers

The pie chart in Fig (2) illustrates quite clearly that the largest part of the claims costs were incurred in accidents involving agency drivers. Only 22.2% of the total outlay was attributable to Rapid's own drivers. Rapid's own drivers did have just over half of all accidents but it would seem that their claims were much less costly for some reason.

CLAIMS COSTS

SPLIT BETWEEN DRIVERS

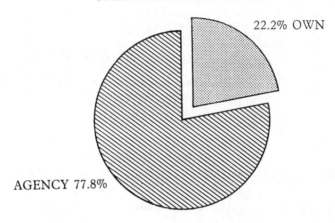

Fig 2

Variability

It is interesting to note that Glasgow depot and agency drivers seem to produce the most costly claims. It will not be a surprise to find that the great majority of Glasgow accidents, 77%, also involved agency drivers.

Glasgow may well represent the largest cost centre for accidents but it has the lowest variability in cost. Fig (3) shows a comparison of average cost against variation as measured by the coefficient of variation. Claims involving Glasgow depot and, not surprisingly, agency drivers have a very low variability in comparison to the very high variability among claims involving Rapid's drivers or a depot like Leeds or London.

CLAIMS COSTS

VARIATION IN COSTS

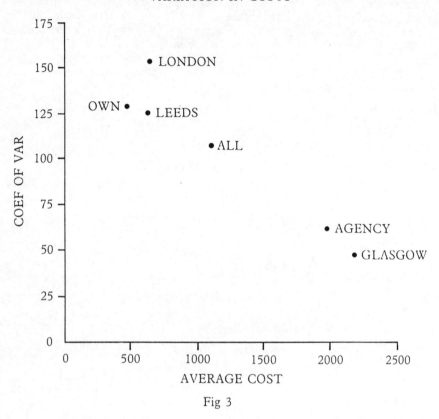

Fig 3

Time

The final figure, Fig 4 (a) and 4 (b), illustrates the time in the year in which the accidents took place. As could be expected, the summer months had the highest number of accidents. What was interesting was that the average cost of claims was much lower in the summer than the winter. The contrast is shown in the two drawings.

Conclusion
- The vast majority of claims are for small to medium size amounts in the range 0 to £1500.

- The Glasgow depot has fewer incidents than the other two depots but they do have the most expensive claims. It would be necessary to know the number of vehicles which operated from each depot in order to comment further on the significance of this.

CLAIMS COSTS

NUMBER OF ACCIDENTS PER MONTH

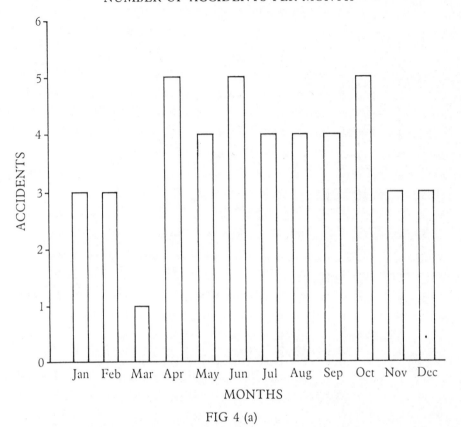

FIG 4 (a)

- Agency drivers have far fewer incidents than Rapid's own drivers but the claims they do have are much more expensive. Again we would need to know the extent of use of agency drivers before being able to comment further.

- The claims from Glasgow and agency drivers are far more tightly grouped around the arithmetic mean cost. This could have important implications for charging premiums to depots in the event of any self funding.

- More accidents take place in the summer than the winter but the winter accidents are much more costly. Enquiries should be made as to when the agency drivers are employed to see if there is any relationship between their use and the rise in cost or number of incidents.

CLAIMS COSTS

AVERAGE COST OF ACCIDENTS PER MONTH

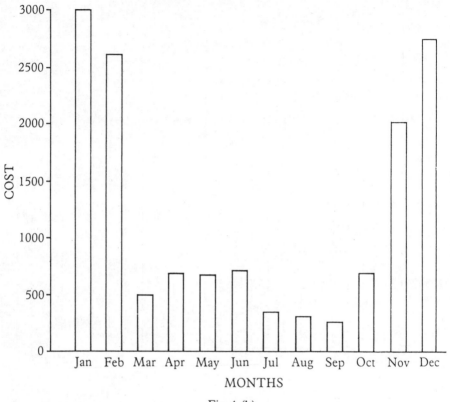

Fig 4 (b)

● The majority of the Glasgow claims involved agency drivers. Enquiries would have to be made to see how many agency drivers are employed at this depot and whether or not it is higher than the other two depots.

This is only an illustration of the shape that a solution to the analysis of the loss experience could take. There are many other ways that the task could have been handled. What is interesting to note is that within this one section of all that is involved in the full case study, we can see that at least two strands of knowledge are called upon. We have the ability to statistically examine a set of raw data and also the skill required in producing a report which summarises the findings. When these two subjects are combined with the legal, behavioural, financial and insurance aspects, which would be required to answer all the issues which arise out of the study, we can see the integration mentioned earlier.

9.2   STICK-RITE ADHESIVES Ltd

You have been the risk manager of STICK-RITE for over three years and during that time have been successful in implementing a reasonably efficient risk management operation. The company is a market leader in the production of industrial solvents and adhesives. It is UK owned but has an association with an American manufacturer of adhesives.

The company has one main manufacturing plant on the outskirts of Birmingham and employs 2,000 people there. There are a number of marketing and sales outlets throughout the country but they are staffed by one or two people at the most. The turnover of the company in the last financial year was £300m. Fifty four percent of the turnover was generated from export sales. The company has been very successful in selling its products in the middle and far east, following a number of sales tours.

The company is now considering an upgrade and possible relocation of their main computer facility. This has come at a time when the company, as a whole, is also reviewing its response to any major disaster on the site. As the risk manager you have been asked for your comments.

The following information about the present premises is available:

THE PREMISES.

Building one.   A large three storey office block of traditional stone-slate construction. There are wooden floors and open stairways. The building is occupied as offices for central administration, management, sales, central planning, the computer centre and the staff canteen. The computer centre is on the top floor.

Building two.   A chemical plant of substantial brick and concrete construction for the manufacture of adhesive raw materials. This forms part of a range of buildings occupied as the power house, transport department and warehouse for packaging and some finished stock. The raw material plant is running at fifty percent capacity. This building also houses the accounts department, personnel and maintenance.

Building three.   This is a new purpose built building which handles adhesive and solvents in bulk. The building is in two sections, the first deals with the bulk adhesive and solvent and the second is a filling and canning operation plus a finished goods area.

As a new building handling large quantities of flammable solvents and other liquids, the fire protection in terms of construction, separation of processes, fire engineering, security and personnel systems are of the highest standard. In the process itself, reliance has been placed on the latest handling techniques backed up by extensive computer control and recording systems. The fire

151

engineering standards at the other two buildings are dated, by comparison, but adequate.

THE COMPUTER

The main computer centre is in building number one, having developed over the years from a modest data processor to a full blown, on-line system. Thirty remote terminals are supported and it is expected that the capacity of the current, recently installed machine, will soon be reached.

The services handled by the computer are order entry, production and despatch, planning, bulk stocks in the warehouse, forecasting, payroll, management information and special projects. The three buildings are all linked to the main computer by land lines. All sales offices throughout the country have access to the main computer system by means of a modem link using the public telephone system.

There are plans to integrate the accounts department with the main computer within the next two years. At the moment the accounts department use a computer agency for the processing of documentation.

The company had a Serious Incident Recovery Plan for the computer and a recent re-appraisal of that plan concluded:

1 The precautions for the disc and tape storage in different buildings was adequate.

2 The advent of on-line systems emphasised the vulnerability of the company in having a computer operation located in a building which, whilst sprinklered and halon protected, contained combustible floors, partitions, a canteen and open stairs.

3 The first stage of the recovery plan was to make use of purpose built portable buildings to house the computer and office staff. It was hoped to have such buildings fitted out with a replacement computer from the manufacturer of the main computer and telephone lines within a few days of any disaster. This plan had been called into question by the United States associate company. They have advised that the computer manufacturer has categorically refused to give any undertaking that a replacement computer could be provided in an emergency.

4 The development of the computer system over the recent past had resulted in a substantial reduction in office staff, this means that any reversion to a manual system would involve employing and training staff.

5 A local computer bureau could be used for some functions but that has serious limitations and is expensive.

6 Duplicated computer hardware located in another building appeared to be the only recommendation which could ensure continuity of the computer service.

Some work has been done to follow up the recommendation in point (6). Three options have emerged from the discussions which have taken place.

Option one   The creation of a computer centre in the part of building two which had been used as a filling plant in the past.

This would involve the transfer of the existing computer (value £300,000), the purchase of a new computer (£410,000) and the location of each computer in adjoining fire proof compartments. The transfer costs are estimated at £95,000.

Option two   A new building in the yard adjacent to building one, to contain the existing and new computers, again arranged in adjoining fire proof compartments. The new building costs are estimated at £350,000. The other costs are the same as option one.

Option three   A new building adjacent to building number three. The costs are the same as for option two. The advantage is seen as placing the new building next to a building which is of a high standard as far as fire protection is concerned.

The two computers have to be close to each other to facilitate parallel running. The computer technicians have said that the distance between the machines must be kept to a minimum.

The problem is that you are now to comment on where you think the computer should be situated, how it should be protected, what the risk management implications of an on-line fully computerised production system would be, what plans should be made for a major emergency on the site involving the computer and what risks emerge during the change over.

9.2.1   At first reading this may seem to be solely a computer study. However, a closer examination reveals that quite a number of different disciplinary areas are involved.

There are five separate issues on which the risk manager is asked for comments:

1. Where should the computer be situated?
2. How should the computer be protected?
3. What risks emerge from an on-line computerised production system?
4. An emergency plan in respect of the computer.
5. What risks arise during the transfer of the computer?

These problems can only be examined by pooling knowledge on:
- fire protection in buildings
- particular systems for protecting computers
- assessing risks arising out of the use of a computer
- understanding production systems
- disaster planning methods
- identification techniques for computer risk analysis.

We can see from this list that no one piece of knowledge will be enough to resolve the several issues which have arisen. The areas of knowledge have to be combined with practical risk management skills and experience.

9.3   QUENCHER plc.

As risk manager for QUENCHER you are responsible for all risk management affairs within the company. Quencher has been in business for over one hundred years and is one of the country's best known names in the soft drink business. It was founded by a chemist in the mid eighteen hundreds and for the first sixty years concentrated on health drinks of all descriptions.

When the last member of the founder's family ceased to be actively involved in the running of the business, a programme of diversification began under the charge of the new managing director. Since then the company has grown considerably and now employs 2500 people at several plants throughout Great Britain. An analysis of last year's annual report shows that the turnover of the group was derived as follows:

Soft Drinks	65%
Health Foods	20%
Ice Cream	10%
Freezer Foods	5%

The company has come a long way from its early beginnings and the managing director has further plans in the pipeline.

You have been employed for ten years and only now feel that you are getting risk management accepted by the various line managers with whom you have to deal. The task has been made more difficult because the last few years have seen rapid growth, both in the company and in the range of products manufactured. The company exports almost twenty percent of its production and this has led to even further problems from the insurance angle. However, in recent months you have detected a willingness to comply with the corporate philosophy on risk management which is contained in a risk management statement issued to all managers.

Just as you feel that matters are gradually coming under control, you receive the following memo:

MEMORANDUM

DATE: 21st January

FROM: James McKenzie; Managing Director

TO: To all on the general management distribution list.

ACQUISITION — "ZESTY Inc."

I am delighted to report that the negotiations for the purchase of Zesty Incorporated of the United States of America have been concluded satisfactorily.

As from one month from today's date, Zesty will become a subsidiary of Quencher. This is clearly a very important day in the history of our company. Up to now, Quencher has been a domestic operation but the purchase of Zesty moves us into a different level of corporate activity with all the challenges and opportunities which this will bring.

Zesty is a major manufacturer of a wine substitute drink aimed primarily at young people and those not wishing to consume traditional wines or spirits. This is a market we have been reviewing in this country for some time and the purchase of Zesty will enable us to open up the market for wine-substitute drinks in the United Kingdom. Moreover it will allow us to do so from the very solid base which that company has built in the United States.

Zesty operates from a corporate headquarters in Pittsburg, Pennsylvania. They have three large distribution warehouses. Once is in Pittsburg, one in Des Moines and the third in Austin. These warehouses are fed with cans and bottles by two canning and bottling plants in Peru. The siting of the plants in Peru is largely historical but they are close to extensive fruit growing areas and sources of relatively low cost labour. A third plant is planned for construction within the next six months but its exact location has not yet been decided.

This acquisition is one of great importance to our company and I would ask you all to ensure that the utmost is done to smooth the integration of Zesty into the existing framework. As a matter of some urgency therefore, would each of you let me know what your level of involvement is likely to be, in this integration exercise.

**James McKenzie
Group Managing Director.**

9.3.1 This is a not uncommon situation in the real world. The range of facts has been kept relatively simple, on purpose, but there is still enough in it to illustrate the nature of the problem facing a risk manager.

Here we have a reasonably large company which is moving into the diversification business in a big way. Not only are they buying a company in a slightly different sector of the market from the parent's operation, they are also buying their first foreign subsidiary and in the process are acquiring operating plants in yet another country.

A number of distinct problem areas emerge:

- The risks arising out of the acquisition.
- The particular issue of international risk management.
- The nature of potential political risks.
- A complete risk analysis of the new, enlarged company.

Each one of these areas is large in its own right and in a situation like this the risk manager has to deal with each one. To answer the managing director's question, the first area listed is probably the most important in the short term.

The risk manager could prepare a note for the managing director which would outline what will be involved in integrating the new operation into the existing risk management structure. Other managers in the company will be concerned with the rationalisation of production, marketing, finance etc. Your job is to give the managing director some idea of what will be involved as far as risk management is concerned.

An outline of a paper you may prepare for the managing director could take the following shape.

Acquisition of Zezty Inc — The Risk Management Perspective

Quencher has established a sound risk management philosophy over recent years and this philosophy now has the support of operating managers throughout the company. The company is beginning to see the benefits of implementing the philosophy, both in terms of reduced risk financing costs and fewer accidents in the workplace.

It would seem important to ensure that this risk management philosophy is extended to embrace the new operation. In other words there is merit in having the risk management function centralised in the UK for the whole, enlarged group. The benefits of this would include:

> *The financial advantages flowing from bulk purchase of covers and services.*
>
> *Central control of risk identification.*
>
> *Simpler liaison with insurers and brokers.*
>
> *Implementation of group-wide risk control procedures.*
>
> *Rationalisation of insurance covers.*

In practical terms the following steps will have to be taken to enable the smooth integration of Zesty into the group's risk management process.

1. *Full details of the company and all its activities are required.*
   The location of all plant, the exact nature of the products produced, an organisational chart if possible and the latest annual report and accounts.

2. *A site visit.*
   It will be necessary to carry out a physical inspection of the premises owned by Zesty, particularly the premises in Peru.

3. *Insurances.*
   A complete schedule of all insurances held by Zesty will be required.

4. *Loss experience.*
   A loss experience schedule will be necessary. We will be interested particularly in any losses arising out of the sale of their product in the United States.

5. *Brokers.*
   Details will be required of the brokers used by Zesty, their remit and any fee arrangements.

6. *Risk control.*
   Any information on loss or risk control procedures implemented by the
   company would be required.

7. *Existing risk management structure.*
   Full details of the existing structure for dealing with risk management will be
   required.

This is only an outline of the points which you may wish to make, as risk manager. There is sufficient here to keep a person busy for some considerable time. Notice, from our point of view, the different disciplines required. A knowledge of insurance is essential as is a knowledge of contract interpretation. Physical inspections are to be carried out requiring skills in that direction. The product liability risk is obviously one which gives concern and a good working knowledge of liability issues would be essential. It will also be necessary to evaluate loss control programmes, take account of existing management structures, study loss records and so on.

This only deals with the first of the issues which the problem creates. There are the other three topics which also arise.

- International risk management
  A host of new issues arise for the risk manager, including consideration of language problems, natural disasters, varying standards of protection, international safety law practice, global covers etc.

- Political risks
  For the first time the company has exposed itself to a range of political risks from which, as a purely domestic operation, it was shielded. These will include consideration of exchange control, governmental stability, kidnap and ransom etc.

- Risk analysis
  Finally, the risk manager has the task of identifying and measuring the risks to which the new, enlarged group is exposed. This may involve a re-think of the risk management philosophy or at the least, the methods by which risks are identified.

9.4   SHINE-IT PLC.

Shine-it PLC is a public company involved in industrial coatings. They have developed a special varnish which can be painted on to most surfaces, eg. wood, plastic, aluminium etc. This new coating of varnish gives the surface an extremely hard and durable finish. There has been a great deal of interest in the varnish, from a wide range of industrial concerns.

The process of applying the varnish is done at the premises of Shine-it. They are working on a version of their new varnish which could be sold to the public for application by them at their own premises. At the moment, however, any customer wanting the varnish applied must deliver the products or components to Shine-it's factory.

The process of applying the varnish is a continuous one. The product is placed on a steel tray which rests on a conveyor belt. The belt moves through a spray booth where the varnish is applied to the product. After this, the steel tray is lifted manually and placed on an asbestos belt which moves through a very hot, dry air drier. It is the application of the dry heat to the wet varnish which actually brings about the very hard surface. The belt moves slowly through the drier and once the product emerges at the other end, it is left to cool. A fire hood covers the drier. The hood has a fan which should operate in the event of a fire. The fan is intended to extract the oxygen from the area and hence extinguish any fire.

Over the past few months there have been a number of small fires when the fan did not always work properly. Shine-it production management fear a major spread of fire from this area of the process. This spread could easily occur if the hood failed to contain any fire which started.

The general manager has asked you to look into the whole question of fire in the factory and to start by examining the possibility of a fire spreading from the drier process to the rest of the plant. He also asks you to extend the investigation into the health and safety field as he is not at all sure that all the possible effects of the fire varnish have been established.

You have investigated the fires which have taken place over the past few months and have found that on the occasions when the varnish ignited, it would seem that excessive varnish or reduced speed on the asbestos belt had been the prime cause. You find this surprising as both the belt and the heat control mechanism have warning buzzers fitted and set to sound. In the case of the belt, the buzzer would have to have failed when the belt had been set at too slow a speed by the operator. The buzzer had been sounding a number of false alarms recently and there was some evidence that operators had been switching it off at the central control. Apart from the chance that the buzzer had been switched off there was also the possibility of electrical or mechanical breakdown.

The warning buzzer on the drier would have to have failed while the drier had been set too high for the varnish. This is thought to be fairly unlikely, but if it did happen the varnish would ignite. The warning buzzer on the drier is intended to give the operator time to take corrective action.

Should the varnish ignite, the hood is intended to contain the fire and it will do so if it is positioned over the belt and it functions properly. Should the hood prove faulty, either because the operator did not switch the fan on or the fan simply malfunctioned, then there would be a problem. The system should allow the operator time to take corrective action in the case of a fan malfunction as a warning light shines at the central control panel. Should the light fail and the fan be faulty, due to mechanical, electrical or material damage, then the fan malfunction could result in a hood fault which in turn may result in any fire not being contained.

In order to respond to the general manager's request that you investigate the whole question of fire in the factory and the particular problem of fire spreading from the drier, you decide to start by carrying out a full investigation of the run of fires which have been taking place. To get to the bottom of the problem you decide that a fault tree should be tried. This would at least highlight the events which could give rise to fire spread.

9.4.1 There would seem to be two main strands of investigation here. There is the question of fire in the factory, with the specific issue of the possibility of fire spread from the drier. Secondly there is the health and safety matter.

On the brief facts given it would seem likely that the growth in activity, following the introduction of the new varnishing process, has overtaken the fire precautions. A full physical inspection would be required and all the risk manager's skill and knowledge in the area of fire engineering would be called upon.

On the specific question of the spread of fire from the drier, the risk manager has already carried out some enquiry and had information which can assist. He has decided that a fault tree would be helpful in illustrating the events which could give rise to a fire spread. A suitable fault tree, based on the facts known, is shown in Fig 1. This is only the start as the risk manager could now add figures of likelihood to the tree and begin the task of ascertaining the most probable set of events which would lead to a fire spreading from the area.

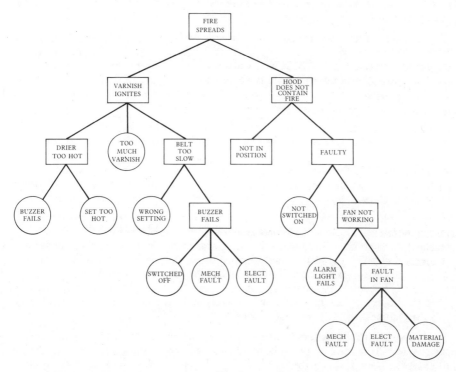

Fig 1

The tree would also be useful when it came to deciding what should be done to minimise the risk of fire spread. If the likelihood of the various events at the root of the tree are known then the risk manager can follow these through to find the chance of a fire spread. He can also plot the effect of any changes ie. let us say that a new hood is available, or a new varnish gun, or extractor fan etc. Each one of these would alter the probability of the main event and what the fault tree allows the risk manager to do is to decide which is most effective in terms of reducing the likelihood of fire spread.

The health and safety matters are of equal importance. In any new process the effect of the various chemicals has to be assessed and monitored. This would involve the risk manager in keeping careful records of all incidents at the factory, their cause, the part of body affected, the process or chemical involved etc. In addition the risk manager, from his own knowledge base or with the assistance of some external help, would want to make some assessment of the long term implications of working with the new chemicals.

9.5   TRADITIONAL HOTELS Ltd.

The Traditional Hotels group has been operating a number of hotels in the United Kingdom many years. The hotel buildings tend to be in city centre situations and cater mainly for business people. Each hotel has a lively trade in their lounge bars and restaurants.

Over the years there has been a steady growth in the volume of thefts of all kinds from the hotel premises. The management of the group has considered this to be a symptom of the age in which we live, but in recent years the level of theft has reached quite alarming proportions. The risk manager has been asked by the general management of the group to look into the whole area of security.

At the moment the hotel group employ the services of a security firm. This company makes regular visits to each hotel, under-cover. They have met with a limited amount of success over the years but do not seem to be hitting at the main problem. The theft risk is insured with a deductible and the premiums have been rising in line with the increase in the number of thefts. The risk manager decided that a complete security survey is called for and he recruits the assistance of a firm of security consultants.

Following the survey a number of recommendations are put forward for immediate implementation. These include measures relating to locks, security checks at staff entrances and so on. There was also one major step which the survey suggested. It seems that the bulk of the thefts involved people opening the doors of rooms with false keys or stolen keys. There was little evidence of forced entry in any of the thefts. The security consultants had worked for a number of hotel groups in the past and one of the most effective methods to deter room thefts had been found to be a change in the type of door lock.

They consider, in the light of their experience, that the modern, card key is a much safer system than the traditional key and lock. The card key is a plastic card issued to guests as they arrive at the hotel. The card fits into the lock on the room door and releases the bolt. The card and door lock can be programmed for each different guest who stays in the room and thus a lost or stolen card would be of no value to a thief.

This is a fairly expensive exercise as all the doors would have to be fitted with the new form of lock and the appropriate hardware would be required to make the plastic keys. As a trial the consultant suggested to the risk manager that one hotel could be selected, which represented the bulk of the hotels in the group, as a sample. After some careful study the risk manager selected one city centre hotel in Manchester, which reflected the bulk of the hotels in the group in terms of age, size, through-put of guests etc.

The cost of the equipment necessary is £20,000. This would have a lifespan of six years, by which time the technology would have changed to such an extent that it would have to be replaced. The benefits of the system are made up of a combination of reduction in thefts, and hence in the amount paid out under the deductible, an eventual lowering of the theft premium as a higher deductible becomes possible in view of the reduction in losses, a reduction in the costs of the security firm as it becomes possible to have less frequent visits by them to the hotel.

It is difficult to forecast these cash savings with one hundred percent accuracy but the best estimate is that the following savings would result:

year		
	1	£2000
	2	£4000
	3	£6000
	4	£8000
	5	£10,000
	6	£12,000

The savings increase over the time scale, as the effect of the measures compound.

The risk manager is now at the point of seeking formal approval for the project to go ahead. Unfortunately, at the same time the property manager for the group also wants to do work at the Manchester hotel. This particular hotel is one of very few which has not been fitted with the latest energy conservation devices for both heating and lighting. The savings following upon the installation of the devices last over a period of five years and relate to a reduction in energy costs. After five years a further review is carried out, with a consequent up-dating of the system.

The cost of installing the energy savings devices, which comprise thermostats, light sensitive switches etc, is £20,000. The savings are expected to be £10,000 in the first year, £7,000 in the second and then £4,000, £3,000 and £2,000 in the third, fourth and fifth years respectively.

The general management of the group sees merit in both projects but is only willing to give financial support to one of them. At the moment the property manager seems to be winning the day as he has been putting forward the point that his project will pay back the capital expenditure in just under three years, while the risk mangement project takes four years to recover the initial outlay. He has also been making the point that the risk management forecasts of saving are highly subjective and in any event the group is insured against the risk of theft, ". . . that is what we pay premiums for!".

Both managers have been asked to make a presentation at a forthcoming finance committee meeting.

9.5.1 This is a classic case of two worthwhile projects and funds for only one of them. The risk manager seems to have his back against the wall. A number of different issues emerge:

- There is the behavioural issue of the property manager being in competition with the risk manager. An understanding of how he perceives risk and risk management will be necessary. It will also be necessary for the risk manager to give some thought to the group dynamics which will be in evidence while the presentations are being made and during the decision making phase.

- There also seems to be a misunderstanding of the role of insurance and some thought will have to be given as to how to overcome this.

- An oral presentation is called for and so skills in this area will be called upon.

- Finally there is the financial appraisal of the two projects. The property manager has taken a rather simplistic view of the investment. Bearing in mind that it is the finance committee which is to receive the presentation, the risk manger will be well advised to prepare a proper, financial analysis of his project.

We can see that once again a range of subject areas are involved. Let us just follow the last point through in order to illustrate the benefit which the risk manager could gain from a full analysis.

There are two projects, each costing £20,000. The cash flows to the hotel are different in each case:

YEAR	PROPERTY PROJECT	RISK PROJECT
1	£10,000	£2,000
2	£7,000	£4,000
3	£4,000	£6,000
4	£3,000	£8,000
5	£2,000	£10,000
6	—	£12,000

What we could now do is to carry out a discounted cash flow analysis of the two projects. Firstly we could calculate the net present value of the future cash savings and secondly we could find the internal rate of return. These are all concepts dealt with in earlier subjects of the Diploma.

Let us assume that the company has set the cost of capital at 10%. In other words the company demands a return of at least 10% on every pound invested. Using 10% as the cost of capital we can now work out the net present value of each project. The calculations are as follows:

PROPERTY PROJECT

YEARS	NET CASH FLOWS £	10% DISCOUNT FACTORS	NET PRESENT VALUES £
0	(20000)	1.000	(20000)
1	10000	0.909	9090
2	7000	0.826	5782
3	4000	0.751	3004
4	3000	0.683	2049
5	2000	0.621	1242
			1167

RISK MANAGEMENT PROJECT

YEARS	NET CASH FLOWS £	10% DISCOUNT FACTORS	NET PRESENT VALUES £
0	(20000)	1.000	(20000)
1	2000	0.909	1818
2	4000	0.826	3304
3	6000	0.751	4506
4	8000	0.683	5464
5	10000	0.621	6210
6	12000	0.564	6768
			————
			8070

We can see from these calculations that the risk management project yields a much higher net present value that the property project. On these grounds alone a case could be made for favouring the new lock project.

The next step would be to find out what the exact rate of return is on each project. This is achieved by the Internal Rate of Return method. What we try to do is to calculate at what rate of interest the net present value of the future cash flow equals the capital sum invested. When this is done for the two projects in this example we find that the property project has a rate of 13.08% and the risk management project, a rate of 19.71%. It is clear from these figures that the risk manager's project has the higher rate of return and hence should be the favoured project. The benefit of this for the risk manager is that it now allows him to put forward the case on objective financial grounds.

9.6   KAR-RITE Plc.

Kar-rite is a car hire company which has been operating in Britain for many years. It hires cars to private individuals and has a network of offices all over the country, including a number of outlets at stations and airport terminals. The company has a fairly aggressive marketing policy and advertises regularly in all sections of the media. Four years ago the company purchased an American car hire company in order to expand its activities into America. The American company had a very similar business profile to Kar-rite and the purchase has been successful in every way.

Until now, the risks arising out of the American operation have been insured in the American market. This has included the accidental damage risk to the fleet of private cars. This has been against the corporate philosophy which is to handle all risk management matters at the corporate head office in London. However, in the light of all the other issues which had to be resolved following the takeover it was decided to leave the motor risk with the American insurer. The company finance director has now turned his attention to the increasing level of the premium being paid for the accidental damage risk and has asked the risk manager to explore the alternatives.

The current method of handling the risk has been for the American operating company to pay the premium on renewal and then submit an account to the corporate head office at the year end and ask for a refund. The refund was made on the last day of the accounting year and the dollar cost was transferred to sterling using the rate of exchange applying on that day. The risk manager knows that the premium this year will be $200,000.

The risk manager has decided that the main alternative to full insurance would be some form of self funding of the accidental damage risk. This is what he does with the British fleet and it has been found to be very successful over many years. In order to get some idea of the losses being sustained by the American company he has drawn a sample of claims and has found the following:

Claims Cost	Frequency
0 <100	70
100 <200	56
200 <300	49
300 <400	31

It is expected that there will be in the order of 1000 claims in the current period. In addition to the uncertainties in the above figures the risk manager is also concerned about the foreign currency risk. He could simply ask the American company to settle all claims as and when they occur and to remit a note of the amount paid at the end of the year. This would be similar to the current method of paying the insurance premium. The British head office would then pay the American company the full amount of the last day of the accounting year and transfer the amount to sterling according to the rate of exchange applying on that day. According to all the advice he can get, there is a fifty percent chance that the dollar will fall in value from its current rate of $1.65 to $1.70 by the year end. The chance of it staying at its present level has been put at forty percent. The only other possibility is that it actually rises in value to $1.80.

In anticipation of the losses he could purchase dollars today for the expected loss amount. An alternative to immediate purchase of dollars would be to buy dollars forward, for the expected loss amount, and have them delivered on the year end. The rate for dollars to be delivered by that day is put at $1.70.

A further complication is that the registered office of the American company is in a State where a licence has to be obtained before an operator of a fleet can self fund losses, even for the accidental risk. It is not certain that a licence would be granted and an unsuccessful application costs £5,000 in management time and effort. The best advice he has is that a first application stands about as much chance of being approved as disapproved.

As the company finance director has asked you to report on the increase in premium costs and the alternatives to the current methods of handling the risk, you have decided to illustrate the structure of the decision for his benefit, and your own.

9.6.1 This is a more straightforward example of a decision problem. There are a number of alternative courses of action and the various probabilities of each outcome are known. Once more there is the need for highly developed report writing skills, in addition to technical knowledge.

The drawing of a decision tree would certainly assist in structuring the decision and in concentrating thought in the right direction. A suitable tree for this problem might take the following shape:

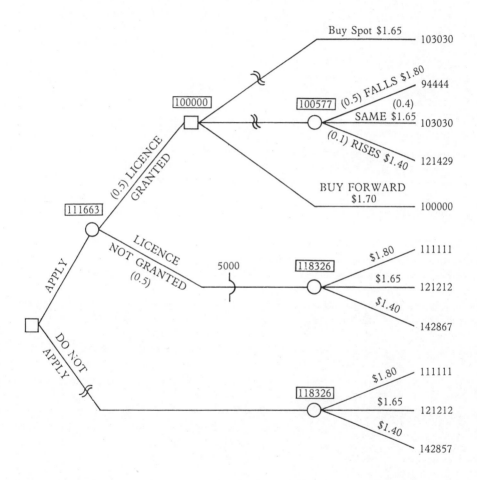

This is only one part of the report which would be required. It does, however provide a structure for the decision and perhaps brings some discipline to the decision process.

A knowledge of how to construct and use these decision trees is obviously essential, as is some understanding of handling foreign currency transactions.

General Index